DANGEROUS PRAYERS FOR THE WORKING OF MIRACLES

DESTINY IMAGE BOOKS BY FRANCIS MYLES

Dangerous Prayers for the Working of Miracles: 40 Prophetic Decrees That Activate Supernatural Breakthrough, Signs, and Wonders

Dangerous Decrees That Destroy Strongholds: Powerful Prayers That Arrest Demons and Crush Satan's Strategies Against Your Life

Dangerous Prayers from the Courts of Heaven That Destroy Evil Altars: Establishing the Legal Framework for Closing Demonic Entryways and Breaking General Chains of Darkness

Following the Footsteps of Rabbi Jesus Into the Courts of Heaven: Partnering with Jesus to Pray Prayers That Hit the Mark

Issuing Divine Restraining Orders from the Courts of Heaven: Restricting and Revoking the Plans of the Enemy (with Robert Henderson)

DANGEROUS PRAYERS FOR THE WORKING OF MIRACLES

40 PROPHETIC DECREES THAT ACTIVATE SUPERNATURAL BREAKTHROUGH, SIGNS, AND WONDERS

DR. FRANCIS MYLES

DESTINY IMAGE® PUBLISHERS, INC.
P.O. Box 310, Shippensburg, PA 17257-0310
"Publishing cutting-edge prophetic resources to supernaturally empower the body of Christ"

This book and all other Destiny Image and Destiny Image Fiction books are available at Christian bookstores and distributors worldwide.

For more information on foreign distributors, call 717-532-3040.
Reach us on the Internet: www.destinyimage.com.

ISBN 13 TP: 979-8-8815-0946-0
ISBN 13 eBook: 979-8-8815-0947-7

For Worldwide Distribution, Printed in the U.S.A.
1 2 3 4 5 6 7 8 / 30 29 28 27 26

CONTENTS

PREFACE

THE WORKING OF MIRACLES

The working of miracles is one of the most awe-inspiring manifestations of the Holy Spirit within the Church. Rooted in the Greek phrase *energemata dynameōn* (1 Corinthians 12:10), it speaks of divine power actively operating through human vessels to accomplish acts that transcend natural laws. These are not human feats, nor mere displays of wonder, but visible proofs of God's living presence—interventions that manifest His glory, confirm His Word, and advance His Kingdom on earth.

Throughout Scripture, the miraculous has always been God's signature on His redemptive mission. The apostle Paul testified that his ministry was marked *"by the power of signs and wonders, by the power of the Spirit of God…"* (Romans 15:19 ESV). Miracles accompanied his preaching as God's confirmation of the gospel, turning hearts toward faith. Similarly, Paul reminded the Galatians that the same God who gave them the Spirit also *"works miracles"* among them—not through works of the Law, but *"by hearing with faith"* (Galatians 3:5 ESV). This underscores a vital truth: *miracles are not relics of a bygone age but present realities wherever the Spirit and faith are active.*

Miracles are initiated by God yet require the cooperation of yielded hearts. They are not conjured by human effort but released through faith—faith that hears God's Word, believes it, and acts upon it. Their purpose is never personal glory or spectacle—they are signs that point to Christ, acts of compassion that meet human need, and demonstrations that the Kingdom of God has drawn near.

This book, *Dangerous Prayers for the Working of Miracles,* explores the spiritual principles and biblical patterns behind the working of miracles. It invites believers to reclaim this vital dimension of Spirit-filled life, not as an occasional phenomenon, but as part of the Church's witness of the living Christ. As the Holy Spirit empowers us and faith rises in our hearts, we become vessels through whom the God of wonders makes Himself known to the world.

Yours for His Kingdom,

Dr. Francis Myles
Author, *Dangerous Prayers from the Courts of Heaven That Destroy Evil Altars*

1

UNDERSTANDING THE GIFT OF MIRACLES

*To another the **working of miracles**, to another prophecy, to another discerning of spirits, to another different kinds of tongues, to another the interpretation of tongues*

(1 Corinthians 12:10 NKJV).

I have for the longest time desired to write a book about *miracles*. It's finally here! By the special grace of God, I have benefitted greatly from the activation of the realm of the miraculous.

The story of my "rising" from abject poverty and sickness to a globally recognized prophetic voice would have been improbable without accessing the realm of miracles. So, I have written this book to explain "eternal mysteries" behind the "working of miracles" followed by powerful and practical prayers of activation!

Miracles are beyond the realm of magic; so like everything God is associated with, miracles are based on a solid rock biblical foundation. The foundation for understanding the gift of the working of miracles begins with understanding their scriptural framework. In 1 Corinthians 12:10, Paul lists *"the working of miracles"* as one of the spiritual gifts distributed by the Holy Spirit. This is not a reference to natural ability, but a supernatural operation given to certain humans as the Spirit wills. In 1 Corinthians 12:10, miracles are grouped with other supernatural manifestations including healing, prophecy, and discerning spirits, emphasizing their divine origin and purpose in the edification of the Church.

> O foolish Galatians! Who has bewitched you that you should not obey the truth, before whose eyes Jesus Christ was clearly portrayed among you as crucified? This only I want to learn from you: Did you receive the Spirit by the works of the law, or by the hearing of faith? Are you so foolish? Having begun in the Spirit, are you now being made perfect by the flesh? Have you suffered so many things in vain—if indeed it was in vain? Therefore ***He who supplies the Spirit to you and works miracles among you***, does He do it by the works of the law, or by the hearing of faith? (Galatians 3:1-5 NKJV)

In Galatians 3:1-5, Paul sharply rebukes the Galatians for departing from the Spirit-led life into religious legalism. He reminds them that *the working of miracles* occurred among them not because of works of the law, but through hearing and believing the Word of faith. This passage teaches us that the miraculous is tied not to human effort or merit but to the operation of faith—believing God's Word and yielding to His Spirit.

Together, these sacred texts reveal that the gift of the working of miracles is both a sovereign distribution and a faith-activated function. However, it is the latter part, faith-activated function of the working of miracles, which is the basis of my writing. I want as many believers as possible to pay the price for this level of the working of miracles. This is what terrifies the devil the most, because it's what we activate by the exercise of our faith that never leaves us. In this way, the working of miracles becomes part of our inherent spiritual DNA.

In Galatians 3:1-5, Paul also warns the Galatians against trying to earn by works what only grace can give. Miracles are not rewards for holiness (even though living a holy life is important), miracles are instruments of divine purpose, working through yielded vessels for God's glory. Will you become one of those yielded vessels for miracles to flow through?

DEFINITION OF MIRACLE IN A BIBLICAL CONTEXT

The term *miracle* often conjures images of the spectacular (such as the dazzling tricks of a magician), but in the biblical sense, the word *miracle* signifies a divine intervention in the natural order of human affairs to accomplish God's purpose. The Greek word used in the New Testament is *dynamis* (δύναμις), often translated as "power" or "mighty work." It implies an act that transcends human ability—God breaking into the natural with His supernatural power. Miracles are the main reason the Bible is very different from other religious books of the most famous world religions.

In the Old Testament, Hebrew words such as *mophet* (wonder) and *oth* (sign) are used interchangeably, emphasizing the function of miracles as "signs pointing to God's reality." A biblical miracle is not just a magical spectacle—it is a divine message, reminding us that the infinitely powerful God does exist. Miracles declare God's sovereignty, His all-consuming presence, and His perfect will. Whether in the supernatural parting of the Red Sea or the raising of the dead, a miracle is a moment when *Heaven invades earth to make God's nature known.*

Miracles also validate the divine messenger (as in Moses or Elijah), confirming the message (as in the Gospels), and meeting our real needs. But more than that, miracles invite observers to the life of faith. *Miracles are signs that point beyond themselves to the God who performs them.*

DIFFERENCE BETWEEN MIRACLES, HEALINGS, SIGNS, AND WONDERS

While the words *miracles, healings, signs,* and *wonders* are often used interchangeably, Scripture distinguishes between them, each serving a unique function in God's Kingdom agenda:

- **Miracles** *(Dynamis):* Acts of divine power that override natural laws—e.g., turning water into wine, walking on water, the raising of Lazarus from the dead. These are displays of God's authority over creation and the land of the dead.
- **Healings** *(Iamaton):* Specific restoration of health to the body or mind. Healing addresses a broken or diseased condition within the body, while a

miracle may include creative acts such restoring a withered limb.

- **Signs** *(Semeion)*: Events that serve as divine markers or confirmations that something supernatural is taking place. "Signs" like the signs on a busy highway point to a truth or validate a person—for instance tongues are a "sign to unbelievers," or Jesus' resurrection as the sign of His identity as the Son of God and God incarnate.
- **Wonders** *(Teras)*: These are acts that provoke awe or amazement, such as tongues of fire seen on the heads of believers on the day of Pentecost (see Acts 2:1-4). A wonder stirs the human soul and disrupts routine perception of the divine. Wonders *(teras)* often combine with "signs" in Scripture, and collectively they create reverence and astonishment.

Each of these words serves a complementary divine purpose. A healing may also be a miracle, such as the healing of the ten lepers! A miracle may be both a wonder and a sign, such as the baptism of fire of believers on the day of Pentecost. However, the distinctions help us appreciate the multifaceted ways God reveals Himself to mankind.

FAITH AS THE CHANNEL: HOW GOD WORKS THROUGH HUMANS BY HIS SPIRIT

> Jesus said to him, "Go; your faith [and confident trust in My power] has made you well." Immediately he regained his sight and began following Jesus on the road (Mark 10:52 AMP).

Without any argument or controversy, *faith is the indispensable channel through which miracles are birthed.* Hebrews 11:6 (NIV) tells us that *"without faith it is impossible to please God."* Faith is not mental assent or positive thinking; it is the spiritual conviction that what God has said is true—and acting accordingly. Western bookstores are littered with books by many famous motivational gurus on the power of positive thinking, but none of their readers or students can work a Bible-based miracle! This is because Bible-based miracles require the worker of the miracle to have absolute faith in God and in God alone!

In Galatians 3:5 (NKJV), Paul connects the supply of the Spirit and the working of miracles with faith: *"He who supplies the Spirit to you and works miracles among you, does He do it by the works of the law, or by the hearing of faith?"* This underscores that the miraculous does not flow through religious ritual or human performance but through believing hearts. Faith positions the believer as a conduit of divine power.

When a man or woman believes what God says and acts on it, the Spirit is free to move. Jesus often said, *"Your faith has made you whole,"* and, *"According to your faith, be it unto you."* Even in His own ministry, Jesus could do no mighty works in Nazareth because of their unbelief (Mark 6:5-6).

A CRIPPLED MAN WALKS!

> Now Peter and John went up together to the temple at the hour of prayer, the ninth hour. And a certain man lame from his mother's womb was carried, whom they laid daily at the gate of the

> temple, which is called Beautiful, to ask alms from those who entered the temple; who, seeing Peter and John about to go into the temple, asked for alms. And fixing his eyes on him, with John, Peter said, "Look at us." So he gave them his attention, expecting to receive something from them. Then Peter said, "Silver and gold I do not have, but what I do have I give you: In the name of Jesus Christ of Nazareth, rise up and walk." And he took him by the right hand and lifted him up, and immediately his feet and ankle bones received strength. So he, leaping up, stood and walked and entered the temple with them—walking, leaping, and praising God (Acts 3:1-8 NKJV).

When I was attending the Hatfield Training Institute at Hatfield Christian Church in Pretoria, South Africa in 1994, I was asked by my college professor to go and assist a church in Mamelodi (a Black Township) that was conducting an evangelistic crusade. I agreed, because the night before I had an encounter with the fire of God, in which the Holy Spirit told me that cripples would begin to walk in my miracle and healing services. So, when the unexpected invitation came, I was ready!

However, when the pastor who was hosting the crusade came to pick me up, he was filled with discouragement and almost stole my faith! The whole way there, he voiced his frustrations with the small attendance at the crusade. Listening to him, I knew why the people weren't coming in large numbers. *Without faith he couldn't enter into the working of miracles.*

I decided to mentally shut him off and began to pray in tongues in my spirit. When we arrived at his church, the driver of a green Toyota Corolla was also pulling into the church parking lot. My spirit was immediately drawn to this car. When the doors of the car opened, one of the passengers was a crippled woman. As I looked at her, the Spirit of God said, "This woman is tonight's major miracle! When you pray for her, she will rise and walk!" I was so excited and very fearful at the same time. Reason—I had never prayed for a crippled person to walk before. I knew the night would both test and stretch my faith for the working of miracles.

That night I preached on "the God who answers by fire." Even though I preached passionately, it was clear that the crowd at the crusade was suffering from the same cloud of doubt that hung heavily on the host pastor. I knew then that the only way to rescue the crusade from total failure was through a miracle.

"They will not listen to you, until you demonstrate my power," the Spirit said. The Spirit of God moved on my heart to ask a bold question, "If I pray for this crippled person and she walks, will you believe in Jesus?"

The somber-looking crowd suddenly came alive and answered in unison, "Yes, we will believe!"

A knot of anxiety tore through my throat, but I knew there was no going back on my bold statement. The crowd was now excitedly animated that something bordering on a miracle was about to happen.

Full of faith in my spirit, but trembling with trepidation, I walked over to the crippled woman. I took away her crutches and put them aside. Then some in the crowd inched in`closer, as some drops of sweat formed on my face. Thinking that working miracles was based on some standardized formula, I picked up the crippled woman and boldly repeated Peter's words to the crippled man who sat at the Gate beautiful before the temple in Jerusalem, "Silver and gold have I none, but such as we have, rise and walk in the name of Jesus of Nazareth!"

Then I waited, for surely the miracle was inevitable now that the "magic" words had come out of my mouth. Minutes later, nothing had happened, except for the fact that the crippled woman was holding onto me tightly. My knees where now having fellowship with each other as fear started creeping upon on my spine and the crowd was getting dangerously anxious.

God in His mercy then threw me a lifeline. "Francis, if you believe that I am going to make this person walk again, why have your hands replaced the physical crutches you threw away? Let go of her now!"

I couldn't believe that the Lord wanted me to become so reckless in my faith! I said to myself, *This crowd will kill me if this woman doesn't walk. Lord, I need a miracle!* Then throwing all caution to the wind, I let go of the crippled woman and then closed my eyes for the inevitable stone throwing that would come my way from the restless crowd.

I heard some women scream as the crippled woman stumbled to stay on her feet—and then I heard cheers as the miracle happened. The crippled woman was walking and then running! The crowd erupted in praise celebrations to Jesus! Tears of joy ran down my cheeks from my eyes!

The most profound miracle, however, was in my heart. I learned a valuable lesson that day about the working of miracles! When my hands let go of the crippled woman, both her and my faith was unleashed! When I stopped imitating her crutches, my faith for

God to heal her was released and hers was as well. That day I learned a very valuable lesson about faith: Faith is not the source of power—God is. *But faith is the access point. It is like a switch that activates a circuit:* the power flows from God, through the believer, to the world.

MIRACLES IN THE OLD TESTAMENT VERSUS NEW TESTAMENT

Miracles occur throughout both Testaments attesting to the supernatural nature of the God of the Bible, but their spiritual context and function reveal progression in God's redemptive plan for mankind.

MIRACLES IN THE OLD TESTAMENT:

In the Old Testament, miracles were often dramatic acts of deliverance, judgment, or supernatural provision—such as parting the Red Sea, fire from Heaven, manna, and water from a rock. These miracles confirmed God's covenant with Israel and authenticated His chosen leaders such as Moses and Elijah. These miracles were typically episodic and connected to Israel's national identity.

MIRACLES IN THE NEW TESTAMENT:

The frequency of miracles increases exponentially in the New Testament, particularly during Jesus' ministry and that of the early Church. Miracles in our modern times have a Christocentric focus—revealing Jesus

(Yeshua) as God's promised Messiah and confirming the gospel message. Jesus' miracles emphasized compassion (such as the healing of the sick), His Sonship authority (such as the commanding of storms), and restoration (such as raising the dead).

A key shift in the New Testament is that miracles are no longer limited to prophets or special leaders, such as apostles. When the Holy Spirit was poured out on *all flesh* (Acts 2:17), the Church became the authorized divine agent of the miraculous. Ordinary believers, empowered by the Spirit, began to work miracles as signs of the arrival of the Kingdom age. This prophetic transition spawned a move from a nation-centered model (Israel) to a Spirit-indwelt, global body—the Church.

THE HOLY SPIRIT AS THE ADMINISTRATOR OF POWER

> Then he said to me, "This [continuous supply of oil] is the word of the Lord to Zerubbabel [prince of Judah], saying, 'Not by might, nor by power, but by My Spirit [of whom the oil is a symbol],' says the Lord of hosts" (Zechariah 4:6 AMP).

At the center of all miraculous activity is the Person of the Holy Spirit. In 1 Corinthians 12:11 (ESV), Paul emphasizes that all the gifts, including miracles, are *"empowered by one and the same Spirit, who apportions to each one individually as he wills."* The Holy Spirit is not merely a force but the divine Person who distributes, directs, and empowers believers to flow in the miraculous.

Jesus Himself performed miracles *"by the Spirit of God"* (Matthew 12:28 ESV). He said, *"The Son can do nothing by himself"* (John 5:19 NIV) pointing to His complete dependence on the Spirit. After His baptism, the Spirit descended upon Jesus, and only then did His miracle ministry begin. It is important for us to note that Jesus, though He was God incarnate, never worked a miracle as God but as a Man totally dependent on the Holy Spirit. This fact alone is the reason believers can work miracles when they completely surrender to the power of the Holy Spirit as Jesus did.

For believers today, the same principle applies. Acts 1:8 (NKJV) promises that *"you shall receive power* [dynamis] *when the Holy Spirit comes upon you…."* The Spirit equips the Church with power, not just for witness, but for supernatural demonstration of God's miracle-working power.

The Holy Spirit is both the Source and Strategist of miracles. He knows the will of God, sees the needs of people, and prompts the believer to act. Sensitivity to the Spirit, therefore, is essential for operating in the gift of miracles. Without Him, there is no divine power, no spiritual accuracy, and no glory to God. This fact alone explains the critical importance of the baptism of the Holy Spirit in the life of every believer.

LIFE APPLICATION SECTION

Memory Verse

O foolish Galatians! Who has bewitched you that you should not obey the truth, before whose eyes Jesus Christ was clearly portrayed among you as crucified? This only I want to learn from you: Did you receive the Spirit by the works of the law, or by the hearing of faith? Are you so foolish? Having begun in the Spirit, are you now being made perfect by the flesh? Have you suffered so many things in vain—if indeed it was in vain? Therefore ***He who supplies the Spirit to you and works miracles among you****, does He do it by the works of the law, or by the hearing of faith?* (Galatians 3:1-5 NKJV)

Reflections

1. Why is faith important in the working of miracles?

____

____

____

____

____

____

____

____

2. What is a miracle?

___

___

___

___

___

___

___

___

___

PRAYER OF ACTIVATION

Heavenly Father, I come boldly before Your throne of grace through the blood of Jesus Christ. I worship You as the God of wonders, the Creator of Heaven and earth, the One who does great and mighty things beyond human comprehension. You are the same yesterday, today, and forever. What You have done, You still do—because Your power never diminishes and Your love never fades.

Lord, I thank You for the Holy Spirit—the Spirit of power (dunamis), the Spirit who raised Jesus from the dead, who now dwells within me. According to 1 Corinthians 12:10 (NKJV), You have ordained "the working of miracles" as one of the gifts of the Spirit. Today, I present myself as a living sacrifice, holy and acceptable to You, and I yield every part of my being to the governance of Your Spirit.

Father, I renounce self-reliance and the works of the flesh. Just as Paul rebuked the Galatians, I will not attempt to earn by works what only grace gives. I choose the hearing of faith. I believe Your Word is true. I believe that Jesus is Lord over creation, disease, death, and all demonic powers. I believe that through the Holy Spirit, You have authorized Your Church—and even me—to carry the power of the Kingdom on earth.

Right now, in the name of Jesus, I activate my faith.

Let the circuit of divine power be switched on in my spirit. I release my fear and doubt. I silence unbelief. I receive boldness. I receive the fire of the Holy Spirit. I receive the mantle of power. Lord, stretch forth Your hand to perform mighty deeds through me—signs, wonders, healings, and miracles—that the name of Jesus may be glorified.

Holy Spirit, breathe upon me—my mind, my hands, my voice, and my spirit. Let the river of Your power flow through me. Teach me to see what the Father is doing, and to act in obedience without hesitation. Make me sensitive to Your promptings and quick to obey. As I go forth, let the sick be healed, the oppressed be delivered, the dead raised, and the lost saved by the demonstration of Your Spirit and power.

Father, I decree that from this day forward, the realm of the miraculous is part of my spiritual DNA. I will walk in faith. I will speak in faith. I will act in faith. And as I do, Heaven will invade earth through my yielded vessel. I will not fear failure, because the power is not mine—it is Yours. I am just the conduit.

Thank You, Lord, for choosing me as a vessel of Your miracle-working power. By faith, I receive the activation of this gift in Jesus' mighty name. Amen.

2

GOD THE CREATOR: THE FOUNDATION OF ALL MIRACLES

In the beginning God created the heavens and the earth. The earth was without form, and void; and darkness was on the face of the deep. And the Spirit of God was hovering over the face of the waters.

Then God said, "Let there be light"; and there was light. And God saw the light, that it was good; and God divided the light from the darkness. God called the light Day, and the darkness He called Night. So the evening and the morning were the first day.

Then God said, "Let there be a firmament in the midst of the waters, and let it divide the waters from the waters." Thus God made the firmament, and divided the waters which were under the firmament from the waters which were above the firmament; and it was so. And God called the firmament Heaven. So the evening and the morning were the second day.

Then God said, "Let the waters under the heavens be gathered together into one place, and let the dry land appear"; and it was so. And God called the dry land Earth, and the gathering together of the waters He called Seas. And God saw that it was good.

Then God said, "Let the earth bring forth grass, the herb that yields seed, and the fruit tree that yields fruit according to its kind, whose seed is in itself, on the earth"; and it was so. And the earth brought forth grass, the herb that yields seed according to its kind, and the tree that yields fruit, whose seed is in itself according to its kind. And God saw that it was good. So the evening and the morning were the third day.

Then God said, "Let there be lights in the firmament of the heavens to divide the day from the night; and let them be for signs and seasons, and for days and years."

(Genesis 1:1-14 NKJV).

"In the beginning, God created the heavens and the earth." These are the opening words of the Bible and the beginning of all miracles and our understanding of them. Genesis 1:1-14 lays the groundwork for every supernatural act that follows in Scripture, from Genesis to Revelation.

Before there were healings, signs, wonders, or deliverances, there was the miracle of creation. "Out of nothing" (*ex nihilo*), God in miraculous symphony spoke the universe with all its vast intricacies into being. His creative act is not only the first miracle—it is the source of all subsequent ones. God's creative act sets Him apart as the ultimate Miracle Worker and Source (Abba) of all miracles. God is the "Father of Miracles," and any supernatural act that is not initiated by Him is nothing less than a lying sign and wonder. The latter is the realm in which all wizards, spiritists, and witches function.

LET THERE BE LIGHT!

This passage, Genesis 1:1-14, demonstrates God's absolute sovereignty over all of creation. God is not bound by time, space, or matter. He speaks, and it is done. When we speak of miracles today, we must understand them in light of the Creator's original work. If God can create the universe with a word, then no healing, deliverance, or provision is too difficult when we rely on the Word of God. God's identity as Creator becomes the foundational reason we can believe in miracles at all. This belief is the cornerstone of the working of miracles.

The first words out of the mouth of the Father of Miracles was, *"Let there be light!"* These words describe the prerequisite spiritual condition that must be present in the spirit of the miracle worker before he or she can operate in the realm of the miraculous. Because the Bible has already told us that the entrance of God's words bring light in Psalm 119:130, New Testament miracle workers must eat a steady diet of God's Word.

The second raw material for the working of miracles that we find in the creation narrative is sound—the spoken word! God did not mentally speak light into being. He verbalized (voiced it) into the atmosphere the miracle He wanted to see! This act alone sets the tone for how miracles happen and what creation responds to. *Miracles are voice-activated spiritual technologies.*

Genesis 1:1-14, also reveals the God of intentionality and order. Each day of creation unfolds with purpose and structure. Light precedes life. Separation prepares for multiplication. Every step is a demonstration of divine wisdom and omnipotence. This passage does not merely inform us about the past—it reveals the character and nature of the God who still works miracles, today.

THE MIRACLE OF CREATION AND GOD'S SOVEREIGNTY OVER THE NATURAL REALM

> Immediately He made His disciples get into the boat and go before Him to the other side, to Bethsaida, while He sent the multitude away. And when He had sent them away, He departed to the mountain to pray. Now when evening came, the boat was in the middle of the sea; and He was alone on the land. Then He saw them straining at rowing, for the wind was against them. Now about the fourth watch of the night He came to them, walking on the sea, and would have passed them by. And when they saw Him walking on the sea, they supposed it was a ghost, and cried out; for they all saw Him and were troubled. But immediately He talked with them and said to them, "Be of good cheer! It is I; do not be afraid." Then He went up into the boat to them, and the wind ceased. And they were greatly amazed in themselves beyond measure, and marveled (Mark 6:45-51 NKJV).

The creation of the world is the supreme display of divine sovereignty. God does not need raw material in order to work miracles. He is not a craftsman using what already exists; He is the Originator of all things. In Genesis, we see His total control over the elements—light, land, water, sky, and vegetation all obey His command. Jesus as the Godman also demonstrated the same supreme display of divine sovereignty over the natural realm when He walked on water, on a very turbulent sea.

God's sovereignty is a crucial theological capstone when considering the subject of miracles. God does not work within nature's limits—He orders and governs it. He is not confined to scientific laws; rather, those laws exist exclusively because He wills them to exist. When God performs a miracle, He is not violating natural law but expressing higher laws of His Kingdom.

Miracles are not interruptions of the course of nature—they are revelations of God's deeper governance over the same. The man or woman who desires to operate in the working of miracles must become acquainted with the idea of God's sovereignty, if they are to believe God for the manifestation of miracles. Understanding this theological capstone makes mountain-moving faith more reasonable and achievable when a yielded vessel cooperates with God. Believing for healing, provision, or supernatural intervention rests on the conviction that God is Lord over space, matter, time, and life itself. Because He can form galaxies with the word of His power, He can certainly intervene in a doctor's report, a financial crisis, or a broken relationship.

THE POWER OF GOD'S WORD TO CREATE

> God...has in these last days spoken to us by His Son, whom He has appointed heir of all things, through whom also He made the worlds;

> who being the brightness of His glory and the express image of His person, and upholding all things by the word of His power, when He had by Himself purged our sins, sat down at the right hand of the Majesty on high (Hebrews 1:1-3 NKJV).

The recurring phrase in Genesis 1—*"And God said"*—is central to our understanding of the working of miracles. God creates and works miracles by His word. Unlike human words, which describe or respond to reality, God's word *produces* reality. When God speaks, things come into existence. *This is not metaphor—it is a miracle.*

Psalm 33:6 (NIV) says, *"By the word of the Lord the heavens were made, their starry host by the breath of his mouth."* Hebrews 11:3 (NKJV) echoes this same truth: *"By faith we understand that the worlds were framed by the word of God...."* God's words carry intrinsic creative power. This principle has vast implications for miracles and those who want to operate in the working of miracles. A poverty of the Word is the reason much of the Church has been robbed of miracles.

When God speaks, healing occurs. When Jesus commanded the storm, it obeyed, instantly. When He said, *"Lazarus, come forth,"* the dead man responded even though four days had passed since His death. Jesus' faith-filled words, *"Lazarus, come forth,"* arrested the decomposition process, reignited his bloodstream, and pulled his spirit back into his body. All of these miracles were actualized by the power of His words. Lazarus stumbled toward the door of the tomb bound in his grave clothes. What we can state conclusively is that *miracles flow from divine utterance.*

As God's image-bearers, when believers align themselves with God's Word—spoken, believed, and declared—they become participants in the miracle-working process. The authority of Scripture and the *rhema* (spoken) word of God continue to release miracles today. Knowing and proclaiming God's promises positions believers to experience His creative power.

PRINCIPLES OF DIVINE ORDER: SEPARATION AND MULTIPLICATION

> Let all things be done decently and in order (1 Corinthians 14:40 NKJV).

Genesis 1 is not chaotic by any stretch of the imagination. It is a masterpiece of divine sequence.

First, there is light (Day 1), then separation (Days 2 and 3), followed by order and population (Days 4 through 6). This reveals three foundational principles of how God works miracles:

1. ORDER:

God does not bless disorder. He prepares the environment before He fills it. Light comes before life. Land appears before plants grow. God sets things in order before release. In terms of the working of miracles, God first takes time to prepare the miracle worker, before He uses him or her to work miracles. This is the reason much of the Church is lacking in the working of miracles, because there are few men and women in the body of Christ who are willing to "submit" to the price of God's dealings in their life.

2. SEPARATION:

God divides light from darkness, waters from sky, land from sea. Separation in Scripture often precedes elevation. God calls out people, places, and things before He blesses them. Another biblical word for *separation* is *consecration.* God will not use the unconsecrated to work His miracle-working power. If you want God to use you in the working of miracles, you must come under the knife of God's consecration. You must be separated from the flesh and all the evil desires of this world. Are you ready for this? If you are, get ready for the working of miracles. Soon enough God will start using you as a human extension of the "rod of God"! (See Exodus 4:20, 17:9.)

3. MULTIPLICATION:

Once order and separation are in place, God commands multiplication. Plants bear seed. Animals reproduce. Humanity is told, *"Be fruitful and multiply."* Once a person who desires to flow in the working of miracles has established divine order and consecration (separation) in their life, the quantity of miracles passing through their life will increase. At this juncture a supernatural atmosphere for miracles will develop like a thick cloud around the yielded vessel.

This divine sequence is mirrored in miracles. When God heals or restores, He often begins by bringing spiritual order—clarity, repentance, alignment—then separates us from what hinders and finally multiplies our fruitfulness in the Kingdom. Miracles are not magic; they follow unshakable divine principles and protocols.

THE MYSTERY OF FAITH IN UNSEEN REALITIES

> By faith we understand that the worlds were framed by the word of God, so that the things which are seen were not made of things which are visible (Hebrews 11:3 NKJV).

Hebrews 11:3 (NIV) declares, *"By faith we understand that the universe was formed at God's command, so that what is seen was not made out of what was visible."* This verse introduces us to one of the great mysteries of faith: believing in the invisible as the source of the visible.

This great mystery of faith shows us that there is an invisible dynamic behind all visible dynamics. In essence, the supernatural world of celestial beings is the "causal realm," and our physical world is the "effect realm." Any worker of miracles who does not understand this vital lesson will be weak in the work of God.

Faith is the "supernatural lens" through which we perceive the miraculous. Without it, the creative acts of God are either myth or metaphor. With it, they become the pattern of divine expectation in our lives. The visible world is not all there is. There is a spirit world where the current laws of physics and thermodynamics are exceeded and transcended. Miracles remind us that reality extends beyond what the eyes can see. I am reminded of the story of Gehazi and the prophet Elisha related to this principle of perceiving invisible reality.

> Therefore he sent horses and chariots and a great army there, and they came by night and surrounded the city. And when the servant of the man of God arose early and went out, there was an army, surrounding the city with horses and chariots. And his servant said to him, "Alas, my master! What shall we do?" So he answered, "Do not fear, for those who are with us are more than those who are with them." And Elisha prayed, and said, "Lord, I pray, open his eyes that he may see." Then the Lord opened the eyes of the young man, and he saw. And behold, the mountain was full of horses and chariots of fire all around Elisha. So when the Syrians came down to him, Elisha prayed to the Lord, and said, "Strike this people, I pray, with blindness." And He struck them with blindness according to the word of Elisha (2 Kings 6:14-18 NKJV).

This is especially relevant in our age of empiricism and science. Faith affirms that what cannot be measured still matters—that God's power works behind the scenes, creating outcomes unseen until the moment of manifestation. The miracle of creation invites us to live with confidence in God's unseen hand. When we pray, believe, and act in faith, we are not escaping reality—we are aligning with a greater one. God's invisible Word created everything we now see. And by that same Word, He continues to create, redeem, and perform miracles today.

Do you now have a deeper understanding of the world of miracles?

I surely hope so!

LIFE APPLICATION SECTION

Memory Verse

By faith we understand that the worlds were framed by the word of God, so that the things which are seen were not made of things which are visible (Hebrews 11:3 NKJV).

Reflections

1. Why is separation or consecration important in the working of miracles?

____
____
____
____
____
____
____
____
____
____

2. How does Genesis 1:1-3 prepare us to work miracles?

____
____

PRAYER OF ACTIVATION

Abba Father, Creator of Heaven and earth, I lift my heart to You, the Father of Miracles, who spoke light into darkness and framed the worlds by the word of Your power. You are the God who calls things that are not as though they were. From nothing, You brought forth everything; and by Your breath, the galaxies still hang in place. You are the Source, the Originator, and the Governor of all creation. Today, I acknowledge Your absolute sovereignty over time, space, matter, and life itself.

Lord Jesus, the Living Word, You walked upon the waters and commanded the winds to cease. You revealed that creation itself bows to Your voice. I worship You as the embodiment of the Father's creative power and the One through whom all things were made. Your Word sustains all things, and Your Spirit animates all life.

Holy Spirit, Spirit of power and creation, I yield my spirit, soul, and body to You. I ask You to brood over me as You did over the waters in the beginning. Let the entrance of Your words bring light into every part of my being (Psalm 119:130). Illuminate my spirit with divine revelation. Cleanse me by Your fire and set my heart apart in consecration for Your use. Establish divine order within me, separate me from all that hinders, and release multiplication of Your works through my life.

Now, in the name of Jesus, I activate faith for the working of miracles.

I silence doubt, unbelief, and fear. I proclaim that miracles are not rare anomalies, but demonstrations of Your Kingdom. I align my voice with Your voice. I choose to speak what You speak. I declare that as I utter Your Word in faith, it shall not return void but will accomplish what You please.

Let there be light! I speak light into dark places. I speak life where there has been death. I speak healing where there has been sickness. I speak abundance where there has been lack. I speak restoration where there has been ruin. By the authority of the name of Jesus and the indwelling power of the Holy Spirit, I decree that the same creative power that birthed the universe flows through me as a yielded vessel today.

Father, clothe me in boldness. Let my eyes be opened like Elisha's servant to see the unseen chariots of fire that surround me. Cause me to live by faith in the invisible realm that governs the visible. From this moment, let Heaven's order govern my words, my hands, and my heart.

I decree and declare: I am a carrier of the Creator's power.

Miracles will flow through me to glorify Jesus Christ. The atmosphere around me will thicken with the cloud of Your glory. The impossible will bow to Your Word in my mouth.

I seal this activation in the name of Jesus Christ. Amen.

3

SUPERNATURAL TRANSLATIONS: DOMINION OVER TIME AND SPACE

And Enoch walked with God; and he was not, for God took him

(Genesis 5:24 NKJV).

Throughout Scripture, there are moments when individuals are suddenly removed from one location to another, bypassing natural laws of time, space, and transportation. These supernatural translations are not metaphorical—they are documented events where God sovereignly suspends the natural order to fulfill divine purposes. In this chapter, we examine three specific examples of supernatural translations and translocations involving Enoch, Elijah, and Philip.

> By faith Enoch was taken away so that he did not see death, "and was not found, because God had taken him"; for before he was taken, he had this testimony, that he pleased God (Hebrews 11:5 NKJV).

Genesis 5:24 (NIV) records that *"Enoch walked faithfully with God; then he was no more, because God took him away."* This is the first recorded instance of a human being supernaturally relocated from earth into Heaven. Hebrews 11:5 affirms that Enoch did not experience death, being "taken up" because he pleased God. This supernatural divine translation reveals that God has complete authority over the boundaries of mortality and time. I am convinced that Enoch's supernatural translation will not be an isolated case, but a model for this kind of miracle for some saints in the last days.

> Then it happened, as they continued on and talked, that suddenly a chariot of fire appeared with horses of fire and separated the two of them; and Elijah went up by a whirlwind into heaven (2 Kings 2:11 NKJV).

Second Kings 2:11 describes Elijah being carried to Heaven in a whirlwind with chariots of fire, bypassing the power of the grave. This miracle happened in front of his faithful disciple and successor, Elisha. Eljah's translation perhaps gives us a glimpse into how Enoch was translated into the heavenly Kingdom.

> Now when they came up out of the water, the Spirit of the Lord caught Philip away, so that the eunuch saw him no more; and he went on his way rejoicing. But Philip was found at Azotus. And passing through, he preached in all the cities till he came to Caesarea (Acts 8:39-40 NKJV).

Acts 8:39-40, is one of my favorite miracles of translocation. The difference between translations and translocations is minuscule, but critical in elevating our understanding of these amazing supernatural phenomena. Translations seem to be Heaven-bound (out of the realm of time and space), whereas translocations are supernatural relocations from one earthly position to another.

Translocations are being reported more in recent years, as God supernaturally transports missionaries from one region or country to the next without passing through a local port of entry or publicly available means of transport. In Acts 8:39-40, Philip is instantly relocated after baptizing the Ethiopian eunuch—he disappears and appears miles away in Azotus.

These events show that time and space are subject to God's command and that geography is no limitation for the Spirit of God. Can you start developing your faith for this kind of Spirit travel? Imagine being supernaturally translocated from the USA to a country in Asia without the hassle of paying hefty air tickets? The possibilities are endless and mind-boggling. When Jesus rose from the dead, translocation became His primary mode of transportation before He was caught up to Heaven in the cloud.

ENOCH AND ELIJAH'S SUPERNATURAL TRANSLATIONS

Enoch's translation was not only an act of divine favor but also a prophetic picture. He walked so closely with God that he did not see death. This miraculous departure speaks to a level of spiritual intimacy that transcends human boundaries. Men and women who want to operate in this realm of the miraculous must be prepared to pay the price of intimacy with the presence of God. Spiritual lukewarmness cannot produce such a personal God encounter. Enoch's translation also foreshadows the future rapture of the Church—a generation that will be caught up without experiencing death.

> Then we who are alive and remain shall be caught up together with them in the clouds to meet the Lord in the air. And thus we shall always be with the Lord (1 Thessalonians 4:17 NKJV).

Elijah's case is more dramatic. Taken up visibly in a chariot of fire, his translation was witnessed by Elisha, who received his prophetic mantle and a double portion of his spirit. Elijah's departure was not just a personal miracle—it marked a transition of prophetic authority. God used it to validate Elisha's new role and to demonstrate that death is not the end for those in covenant with Him. Since God promised to send the spirit of Elijah to New Testament believers, it implies this supernatural dimension for translations will become an impending possibility in the last days before the second coming of Jesus Christ.

Both of these examples illustrate that God is not bound by the laws of physics. He can bypass decay, override mortality, and transport His servants at will. These miraculous acts remind us that God's Kingdom is above the natural realm, and those who walk closely with Him are not limited by earthly constraints. Spiritual knowledge like this makes possible the working of miracles.

PHILIP'S GEOGRAPHICAL TRANSLATION

> Now when they came up out of the water, the Spirit of the Lord caught Philip away, so that the eunuch saw him no more; and he went on his way rejoicing. But Philip was found at Azotus. And passing through, he preached in all the cities till he came to Caesarea (Acts 8:39-40 NKJV).

Philip's supernatural relocation in Acts 8:39-40 is a unique New Testament example of divine transportation. After baptizing the Ethiopian eunuch, *"the Spirit of the Lord caught Philip away."* The word used here, *harpazo,* is the same used in 1 Thessalonians 4:17 for "caught up" in reference to the rapture. Philip was physically moved from one place to another—instantaneously and miraculously.

The Ethiopian eunuch, who experienced this miracle firsthand was amazed and burst out in worship and adoration of God. This means that though the supernatural translocation of Philip was supernatural, it did not feel like magic or witchcraft. The Ethiopian eunuch knew intuitively that it was a marvelous act of God.

This supernatural translocation (translation) served both evangelistic and logistical purposes. It showed that the Spirit directs ministry and that time and distance are no obstacles to God's redemptive plan. Philip's obedience positioned him to be used beyond his natural capacity. Philip's reaction when the Spirit of God dropped him in Azotus shows us that he was used to this kind of supernatural travel.

This supernatural translocation (translation) also serves as a lesson in spiritual availability. When we yield to the Spirit, and are available for His use; He can accelerate our influence, multiply our reach, and move us supernaturally into divine appointments. While such translations may not be normal (common), they reveal the extent of the Spirit's power and the availability of extraordinary intervention in human affairs.

SPIRITUAL REALMS INTERSECTING WITH THE NATURAL

> Esteeming the reproach of Christ greater riches than the treasures in Egypt; for he looked to the reward. By faith he forsook Egypt, not fearing the wrath of the king; for he endured as seeing Him who is invisible (Hebrews 11:26-27 NKJV).

All these supernatural events point to a deeper truth: the spiritual realm is not separate from the physical—it intersects with it constantly. What we call a "miracle" is often just the visible manifestation of invisible spiritual dynamics governed by superior laws of the Kingdom. God's throne, angelic activity, and spiritual laws are as real as gravity, even if unseen.

Translation (translocation) miracles like those of Enoch, Elijah, and Philip show that Heaven can touch earth at any time. The boundary between Heaven and earth is thin when faith and divine purpose align. Scripture repeatedly affirms that the natural world is upheld by spiritual laws and realities (Hebrews 1:3). In moments of divine translation, the veil is pulled back, and God's superior dimension is revealed.

Understanding this unbreakable reality helps believers live with heightened spiritual awareness. Prayer, worship, and obedience are not mere rituals—they are interactions with a supernatural realm more real than what we see. These supernatural accounts that we have studied awaken a hunger for greater sensitivity to God's movements and remind us that our world is infused with unlimited spiritual potential.

DIVINE AUTHORITY OVER TIME, MATTER, AND SPACE

> Then Joshua spoke to the Lord in the day when the Lord delivered up the Amorites before the children of Israel, and he said in the sight of Israel: "Sun, stand still over Gibeon; and Moon, in the Valley of Aijalon." So the sun stood still, and the moon stopped, till the people had revenge upon their enemies. Is this not written in the Book of Jasher? So the sun stood still in the midst of heaven, and did not hasten to go down for about a whole day. And there has been no day like that, before it or after it, that the Lord heeded the voice of a man; for the Lord fought for Israel (Joshua 10:12-14 NKJV).

Supernatural translations demonstrate God's total dominion over creation. He governs time, commands matter, and overrides distance. For Him, moving someone across a nation or lifting them into eternity requires no more effort than speaking a word. We must never forget that time is a created dimension, and God exists beyond it. All matter is subject to His voice, and space poses no barrier to His divine will and counsel. These truths should not only stir awe—they should also ignite boldness. Because God can relocate a prophet or evangelist without delay, then surely, He can orchestrate divine timing in our lives.

These miraculous accounts affirm that God is not only the Creator but the continual Sustainer and Intervener in our world. He is not a distant deity but an active, all-powerful Lord who rules the laws of nature rather than being subject to them. His authority over time, matter, and space means He can accelerate outcomes, restore lost time, and move His people into destiny with supernatural precision. When we understand that God holds time and space in His hand, our prayers change. Our expectations grow. And our faith rises to believe that, even in the constraints of the natural world, we serve the God who is unlimited by it. Are you ready for miraculous translations or translocations? Get ready, one of these days you might catch one!

LIFE APPLICATION SECTION

Memory Verse

Now when they came up out of the water, the Spirit of the Lord caught Philip away, so that the eunuch saw him no more; and he went on his way rejoicing. But Philip was found at Azotus. And passing through, he preached in all the cities till he came to Caesarea (Acts 8:39-40 NKJV).

Reflections

1. What happened to Philip when he finished baptizing the Ethiopian eunuch?

2. Can we work miracles over nature?

PRAYER OF ACTIVATION

Abba Father, Creator of time, space, and matter, I worship You—the God who "upholds all things by the word of His power." You translated Enoch, caught Elijah up in the whirlwind of Your glory, and snatched Philip to Azotus by the Spirit. You are Lord over distances, schedules, borders, and bodies; nothing restrains You from saving by many or by few.

Lord Jesus Christ, the Living Word, You walked upon the waves and appeared in locked rooms after Your resurrection. By Your blood I have access to the throne of grace. I confess that You are sovereign King; Your Kingdom's laws supersede natural law. I submit my mind to Your truth and my will to Your command.

Holy Spirit, Lord and Giver of Life, brood over me as You brooded over the waters in the beginning. Bring light into every dark place within me—"Let there be light!" Consecrate my heart; separate me from unbelief, pride, and compromise. Establish divine order in my life; then multiply Your works through my hands for the glory of Jesus.

I make these renunciations and confessions:

- *I renounce all counterfeit and occult arts—every "lying sign and wonder." I cleave to the Father of Miracles alone.*
- *I reject fear, fatalism, and fleshly striving. I choose the hearing of faith.*
- *I embrace intimacy like Enoch, obedience like Philip, and prophetic zeal like Elijah.*

By faith, I activate the gift of the working of miracles.

In Jesus' name, I receive boldness to obey instant promptings of the Spirit. I present my body as an instrument of righteousness—my feet for divine appointments, my voice for divine utterance, my hands for impartation. Let angelic help be assigned according to Your Word. Let timing be accelerated, routes be opened, and divine logistics be ordered for gospel purposes and the edification of the Church.

I decree by the authority of Jesus' name:

- *The God who translated Enoch governs my beginnings and endings; death and time have no dominion over Your purpose for me.*
- *The mantle of Elijah confirms transitions of authority in my life and ministry; let whirlwinds of Your glory carry Your agenda forward.*
- *As with Philip, the Spirit directs my steps; I am positioned, repositioned, and "found" where Your harvest waits.*
- *Like Joshua, I ask and expect Heaven's alignment with earth's battles; Lord, command the "sun" and the "moon" of my circumstances according to Your will.*

Father, let my tongue agree with Your Word.

I command confusion to lift, winds to still, and obstacles to move as I speak Scripture in faith. Frame my days by Your rhema; make my schedule submit to Your sovereignty. Translate me—from fear to faith, from delay to divine timing, from limitation to Spirit-led mobility. Whether by ordinary paths or extraordinary interventions, place me precisely where Your glory must be revealed.

I consecrate my life for holy assignments.

Keep me humble, pure, and alert. Guard me from presumption; anchor me in Scripture, counsel, and fruit that glorifies Christ. Let every manifestation authenticate Your message, advance Your gospel, and comfort Your people.

Now, O Lord, perform Your Word.

Thicken the atmosphere around me with Your presence. Let testimonies arise of supernatural deliverance, strategic relocations, and God-timed encounters. Make me a faithful witness to the powers of the age to come.

I seal this activation in the name of the Father, and of the Son, and of the Holy Spirit. Amen.

4

DIVINE INTERVENTION IN HUMAN INABILITY

And the Lord visited Sarah as He had said, and the Lord did for Sarah as He had spoken. For Sarah conceived and bore Abraham a son in his old age, at the set time of which God had spoken to him. And Abraham called the name of his son who was born to him—whom Sarah bore to him—Isaac. Then Abraham circumcised his son Isaac when he was eight days old, as God had commanded him. Now Abraham was one hundred years old when his son Isaac was born to him. And Sarah said, "God has made me laugh, and all who hear will laugh with me." She also said, "Who would have said to Abraham that Sarah would nurse children? For I have borne him a son in his old age"

(Genesis 21:1-7 NKJV).

Faith is not just a theological concept—it is the engine behind the miraculous. From the first book of the Bible to the New Testament letters, faith is repeatedly shown as the means by which the impossible becomes reality. Three pivotal passages demonstrate this: (1) the birth of Isaac in Genesis 21:1-7; (2) Abraham's unwavering belief in Romans 4; and (3) the miraculous multiplication of oil on behalf of a widow woman in 2 Kings 4.

These stories span different time periods and needs—conception, provision, and resurrection of hope—but the common thread is the unwavering belief in God's ability to perform what He had promised. Whether in the womb of a barren woman or the empty jars of a destitute widow, God's power meets human faith to produce supernatural results. It is absolutely critical for all workers of miracles to never forget this fact. If they pierce God's supernatural realm with the unshakable hand of faith, a touch back from God is almost inevitable.

THE CONCEPTION OF ISAAC

Genesis 21:1-7 records the fulfillment of a 25-year-old promise: the birth of Isaac. Abraham was 100 years old, and Sarah was well past childbearing age. She was well past her menopause and yet, God's word came to pass. *"The Lord visited Sarah as He had said, and the Lord did for Sarah as He had spoken."* This statement emphasizes the faithfulness of God's word—it does not return void. This fact by itself should embolden all miracle workers and people of faith. Because God said it, He will make it good!

The miracle of Isaac's birth was not just biological—it was prophetic. It established the lineage of promise through which the Messiah would eventually come. Sarah's laughter, initially filled with doubt, turned into joyful praise, when she held Isaac in her arms. This miracle reveals that time and physical limitations are no hindrance to God. God will work His miracles just the same.

Isaac's conception teaches us that when God speaks, He also empowers everything and everyone connected to the fulfilment of His word. God's word carries the ability to override both natural laws and chemical or biological constitution. Miracles often begin with a promise and are fulfilled through patient, persevering faith.

MULTIPLICATION OF THE WIDOW'S OIL

> A certain woman of the wives of the sons of the prophets cried out to Elisha, saying, "Your servant my husband is dead, and you know that your servant feared the Lord. And the creditor is coming to take my two sons to be his slaves." So Elisha said to her, "What shall I do for you? Tell me, what do you have in the house?" And she said, "Your maidservant has nothing in the house but a jar of oil." Then he said, "Go, borrow vessels from everywhere, from all your neighbors—empty vessels; do not gather just a few. And when you have come in, you shall shut the door behind you and your sons; then pour it into all those vessels, and set aside the full ones." So she went from him and shut the door behind her and her sons, who brought the vessels to her; and she poured it out. Now it came to pass, when the vessels were full, that she said to her son, "Bring me another vessel." And he said to her, "There is

> not another vessel." So the oil ceased. Then she came and told the man of God. And he said, "Go, sell the oil and pay your debt; and you and your sons live on the rest" (2 Kings 4:1-7 NKJV).

In 2 Kings 4:1-7, a widow of one of the sons of the prophets is in desperate financial need. Her sons were about to be taken as slaves to satisfy a debt their father had left unpaid. Thankfully, she knew that one of the vehicles God uses for the working of miracles is a man or woman who sits in a bona fide prophetic office. Elisha asked the widow woman about what she had in her house. Her immediate reply is telling: "Nothing except a jar of oil." What she saw as insignificant became the vessel of her miracle. We must be careful not to marginalize anything in the realm of miracles.

The prophet Elisha instructs her to borrow empty vessels from her neighbors and pour out "into them" what she had in her jar of oil. As she pours, the oil multiplies until every borrowed container is full. Then the oil stops. Here is a critical principle that governs the working of miracles. I call this *the principle of capacity.* The supernatural release of oil continued until she had no more empty vessels (maximized her capacity).

The oil miracle was proportionate to her obedience (faith) and the number of vessels she provided. This prophetic account of the widow woman teaches us that God meets us at the point of our obedience or faith. The oil did not multiply while sitting still—it multiplied as it was poured. Faith is action. God used what was in her house to provide for her future. Her limitation became the stage for God's abundance. God used her limitation to demonstrate His miracle-working power.

GOD'S POWER MANIFESTS IN HUMAN WEAKNESS

> (As it is written, "I have made you a father of many nations") in the presence of Him whom he believed—God, who gives life to the dead and calls those things which do not exist as though they did; who, contrary to hope, in hope believed, so that he became the father of many nations, according to what was spoken, "So shall your descendants be." And not being weak in faith, he did not consider his own body, already dead (since he was about a hundred years old), and the deadness of Sarah's womb. He did not waver at the promise of God through unbelief, but was strengthened in faith, giving glory to God (Romans 4:17-20 NKJV).

Both the conception of Isaac and the multiplication of oil reveal a profound spiritual truth: *God's power is made perfect in weakness.* Romans 4:20 (NIV), highlights Abraham's faith, noting that *"he did not waver through unbelief regarding the promise of God, but was strengthened in his faith and gave glory to God."*

The primary reason God's power is made perfect in weakness is due to the fact that God is determined that no flesh should glory in His presence. Our flesh, though fallen and dangerously corrupt, loves to glory it its own strength. If Abraham and Sarah had given birth to Isaac when they were relatively young, there would have been no Romans 4:17-19. The credit would have gone to their well-oiled biological bodies; and just like that, one of the greatest supernatural testimonies of childbirth would have been lost to history.

According to Romans 4:17-20, Abraham considered his own body *"as good as dead,"* yet believed God's promise. God often chooses the unlikely and the incapable to demonstrate His infinite glory. Weakness is not a disqualification—it is the very platform God uses to showcase His mighty power. The greater the weakness, the clearer the miracle. In the widow's case, her lack became the context for supernatural overflow.

In Sarah's case, her barrenness became the stage for life as being raised from the dead. Faith does not ignore weakness, it acknowledges it while trusting in God's strength. Miracles are not for the qualified—they are for yielded vessels and thoroughly surrendered. These men and women can be easily guided by the symphonic movements of the Holy Spirit into rivers of living waters.

FAITH THAT CALLS THINGS WHICH DO NOT EXIST AS THOUGH THEY DID!

> (As it is written, "I have made you a father of many nations") in the presence of Him whom he believed—God, who gives life to the dead and calls those things which do not exist as though they did; (Romans 4:17 NKJV).

Romans 4:17 describes God as the One who gives life to the dead and calls into being things that are not as though they truly exist. This is the essence of faith: seeing what God sees and declaring it before it is visible. Abraham believed in God's creative power—the ability to bring life from death and substance from nothing. This kind of faith aligns with God's inherent nature. Just as God spoke light into darkness in Genesis 1, Abraham learned to speak "God's promise" into barrenness that overshadowed his body and Sarah's.

This principle of calling things that be not (Romans 4:17 King James Version) is vital for operating in the miraculous. Faith does not wait for proof to believe, it believes and then sees. Hebrews 11:1 (NKJV) calls faith *"the substance of things hoped for, the evidence of things not seen."* Speaking what God has promised—even when reality contradicts it—is not denial of the facts, it is divine alignment. When believers dare to speak the unseen, they partner with God's creative process. The womb responds. The oil multiplies. The impossible bows to the God's words. Faith that calls things that are not as though they were, is the catalyst of miracles.

These Bible stories remind us that God is not looking for perfection in the human condition before He works miracles. God just waits for faith to appear before He starts moving. When we bring our emptiness, our weakness, and our hope to Him, He fills, strengthens, and fulfills. The God who gave a son to the barren and overflowed the oil of the desperate still responds to faith today. The same creative Word that formed the world is still at work—waiting for someone to believe for the working of miracles.

LIFE APPLICATION SECTION

MEMORY VERSE

(As it is written, "I have made you a father of many nations") in the presence of Him whom he believed—God, who gives life to the dead and calls those things which do not exist as though they did; (Romans 4:17 NKJV).

REFLECTIONS

1. In the working of miracles, why is it important to call those things that be not as though they exist?

2. What instruction did the prophet Elisha give the widow woman to activate her miracle?

PRAYER OF ACTIVATION

Heavenly Father, I worship You as the God who cannot lie, the faithful Covenant Keeper who calls things that are not as though they were. You spoke worlds into being and uphold all things by the word of Your power. You visited barren Sarah and she conceived. You multiplied the widow's oil until every vessel overflowed. You strengthened Abraham's faith until he became the father of many nations. You are the God of the impossible, and there is nothing too hard for You.

Lord Jesus Christ, You are the Living Word made flesh. You are the "Yes" and "Amen" to every promise of God. Your miracles proved that the power of God flows where faith is present. Today, I confess that You are my Source, my Sufficiency, and my only Hope. I cling to Your promises, for they are life to my bones and light to my path.

Holy Spirit, Spirit of Faith and Power, I invite You to overshadow my heart as You overshadowed the virgin womb of Mary. Infuse me with unshakable trust in the Father's Word. Burn away the residue of unbelief, fear, and human reasoning. Let the fire of faith erupt in my spirit until I dare to believe for what has never been seen. Teach me to perceive weakness not as disqualification, but as the stage for Your glory. Where I am barren, create life. Where I am empty, pour oil. Where I am broken, release resurrection power.

By faith, I now activate the realm of the miraculous in my life.

I choose to believe before I see. I will not waver at the promise of God through unbelief, but I will grow strong in faith, giving glory to God. I align my tongue with Your truth:

- *I call forth abundance where there is lack.*
- *I call forth life where there is death.*
- *I call forth restoration where there is loss.*
- *I call forth strength where there is weakness.*

Like Abraham, I will not consider the deadness of natural circumstances. Like Sarah, I will laugh at impossibilities when Your promise comes to pass. Like the widow, I will pour out what I have in obedience until every vessel You send me is full.

Father, let this be written in my spiritual DNA: Faith is the engine that pulls the train of miracles. From this day forward, I walk by faith and not by sight. I decree that Your word in my mouth will manifest what Your Spirit has conceived in my heart. As

I move in obedience, miracles will multiply, promises will manifest, and Your glory will be revealed through my yielded vessel.

I seal this activation in the name of Jesus Christ. Amen.

5

FIRE, BUSHES, AND RODS: MIRACLES IN THE CALL OF MOSES

Now Moses was tending the flock of Jethro his father-in-law, the priest of Midian. And he led the flock to the back of the desert, and came to Horeb, the mountain of God. And the Angel of the Lord appeared to him in a flame of fire from the midst of a bush. So he looked, and behold, the bush was burning with fire, but the bush was not consumed. Then Moses said, "I will now turn aside and see this great sight, why the bush does not burn." So when the Lord saw that he turned aside to look, God called to him from the midst of the bush and said, "Moses, Moses!" And he said, "Here I am"

(Exodus 3:1-4 NKJV).

The call of Moses is marked by extraordinary miracles that serve not only to amaze but to affirm the power of divine calling and ordination. In Exodus chapters 3 and 4, God reveals Himself through supernatural phenomena: a green-leaved bush that burns without being consumed, this initial miracle that caused Moses to turn and face God was followed by more spectacular miracles. Namely, an ordinary rod (shepherd's stick) that turns into a serpent, and a hand that becomes leprous and is then supernaturally restored. Each of these miraculous signs carries profound symbolism and theological depth, providing insight into how God uses miracles not just as acts of power and supremacy, but as means of communicating His eternal purpose.

These miraculous encounters form the foundation of Moses' prophetic commission and apostolic ministry. They do not simply serve as human attention-grabbers; they are revelations of God's divine nature and assurances of what having His glorious presence entails for all of us. Moses' hesitation and self-doubt was met with supernatural demonstrations that God is both the Sender of His special messengers and the Source of everything they will ever need.

These miracles that God demonstrated before Moses gave weight to the divine mandate upon his life. They also foreshadowed the greater miraculous signs that would follow his ministry in Egypt and beyond. Without a shadow of doubt, Moses is the greatest delegated authority of God in the Old Testament. He was also the most used in the working of miracles by God. So his life is a true prophetic template for the working of miracles.

ORIENTATION FOR MIRACLES

The prevailing principle that I want you to adopt from Moses' story is the fact that God has never used anyone in the working of miracles who has not been indoctrinated or introduced to the world of the supernatural. God first initiates His special miracle workers by serving them a diet of an ever-growing stream of divine encounters and glory consciousness.

These divine encounters are also designed to alter the spiritual consciousness of the human vessels God desires to use in the working of miracles. Most importantly, these divine encounters are designed to increase the level of death to the flesh in people God wants to use. For there is no greater enemy to the work of God than the "flesh and a carnal mind."

> For those who live according to the flesh set their minds on the things of the flesh, but those who live according to the Spirit, the things of the Spirit. For to be carnally minded is death, but to be spiritually minded is life and peace. Because the carnal mind is enmity against God; for it is not subject to the law of God, nor indeed can be. So then, ***those who are in the flesh cannot please God*** (Romans 8:5-8 NKJV).

The passage of Scripture from Romans 8:5-8 gives us two "demonically engineered" programs that are violently opposed to living out the life of the Spirit, namely, the "flesh" and the "carnal mind."

The first program "the flesh" is driven by the fallen nature of Adam and it compels people to move in the direction of their fleshly or worldly desires. Our primal (animal) instinct dictates the order of the day in the lives of people controlled by the flesh. They are completely blind to the world of the supernatural as it relates to the Person of God. At best they only acknowledge the "demonic supernatural" while stating emphatically that God does not exist.

The second program, "the carnal mind" is primarily driven by the fragmented soul of fallen mankind on three axles: "will, mind, and emotions." The mind is the intermediary agency of the soul bridging the will and emotions, determining under different stimuli which will prevail, will or emotions. In most humans, emotions pretty much drive the whole house. It is no wonder being carnally minded is death.

GOD REVEALS HIMSELF IN FIRE WITHOUT CONSUMPTION

> Now Moses was tending the flock of Jethro his father-in-law, the priest of Midian. And he led the flock to the back of the desert, and came to Horeb, the mountain of God. And the Angel of the Lord appeared to him in a flame of fire from the midst of a bush. So he looked, and behold, the bush was burning with fire, but the bush was not consumed. Then Moses said, "I will now turn aside and see this great sight, why the bush does not burn." So when the Lord saw that he turned aside to look, God called to him from the midst of the bush and said, "Moses, Moses!" And he said, "Here I am" (Exodus 3:1-4 NKJV).

The third chapter of Exodus opens with Moses tending sheep in the wilderness—a place of isolation and obscurity. Interestingly enough, most miracle workers went through intensive seasons of isolation and obscurity as God was separating them to Himself, while chiseling their character.

Suddenly, Moses sees a bush engulfed in flames, yet it was not consumed. This divine paradox captured his attention and became the stage for a divine encounter. Fire, in Scripture, often symbolizes God's presence, purity, and power. You cannot become a bona fide miracle worker if you refuse to be purified by fire! But in Moses's case, it also speaks of divine preservation—God's supernatural ability to burn without destruction. The burning bush is therefore a prophetic symbol of what happens to us when we "catch the fire" of His presence. We will "burn" while God invites millions to "watch us burn"!

The burning bush also represented Israel: oppressed but not destroyed, persecuted but divinely preserved. It also speaks of divine holiness. Holiness is the standard God expects to be maintained by those who desire to participate in the working of miracles. When God calls Moses by name, He instructs him to remove his sandals because he was standing on holy ground. His sandals represented his walk apart from the holy fire of consecration. God's fiery presence is not casual—it demands worshipful reverence, before we dare approach.

Yet it is also invitational; God initiates this moment to commission Moses for the deliverance of His people. God has to personally commission His miracle workers. We must first be sent to truly represent God and His eternal purposes! Those who just go inevitably burn out and, more often than not, are captured by the demonic powers. God is only responsible for protecting the ones He has sent from the crucible of His purifying fire!

The miracle of the burning bush teaches us that God's presence is both powerful and preserving. He reveals Himself not in destruction but in sanctifying fire. When God calls, He brings clarity and awe, drawing the ordinary into the extraordinary and divine purpose.

Such was my case, when the glory of God showed up in my room, while I was living in a shanty town in Zambia called Chimwemwe (which means *joy*, in my language). The light of God's glory went through my whole being while I slept. It unzipped my body like a piece of luggage. I found my spirit standing next to my lifeless body, even though I knew I was not dying. What happened next left an indelible mark on my life! I was wasted for His presence soon after. The hunger to walk in the supernatural consumed my very being! *I am still hungry for more!*

MOSES' ROD BECOMES A SERPENT

> And He said, "Cast it on the ground." So he cast it on the ground, and it became a serpent; and Moses fled from it. Then the Lord said to Moses, "Reach out your hand and take it by the tail" (and he reached out his hand and caught it, and it became a rod in his hand), "that they may believe that the Lord God of their fathers, the God of Abraham, the God of Isaac, and the God of Jacob, has appeared to you" (Exodus 4:3-5 NKJV).

In the fourth chapter of Exodus, Moses expresses doubt about his ability to convince the Israelites and confront Pharaoh. In response, God gives him two miraculous signs. First, He instructs Moses to throw his shepherd's rod on the ground. It became a serpent, and Moses ran away from it. God then commands him to pick it up by the tail—an act of courage and absolute trust in God. Anyone skilled at the art of handling snakes, knows how dangerous it is to catch a snake by its tail instead of its head. As Moses obeys, his shepherd's rod returns to its original form.

This prophetic sign is layered with meaning. The rod represents Moses' identity as a shepherd—a symbol of his current vocation and status. When cast down, it becomes a serpent—perhaps alluding to Egypt and Pharaoh's power, often associated with serpents. The crown of the Pharaohs always had the head of serpent at the apex of the crown. Thankfully, when Moses obeyed God's instruction and takes it up again, it returns to being a rod. This shows us that what is surrendered to God can be transformed and used for divine purposes. I also believe the serpent also represents our sinful nature, untouched by the power of God.

MOSES' HAND BECOMES LEPROUS

> Furthermore, the Lord said to him, "Now put your hand in your bosom." And he put his hand in his bosom, and when he took it out, behold, his hand was leprous, like snow. And He said, "Put your hand in your bosom again." So, he put his hand in his bosom again, and drew it out of his bosom, and behold, it was restored like his other flesh (Exodus 4:6-7 NKJV).

The second sign is even more personal. God tells Moses to place his hand inside his cloak. When he pulls it out, it is leprous—white and diseased. He puts it back in, and it is restored to a healthy hand. This act reveals God's authority over human health and affliction. It also symbolizes the human condition without God—corruption and moral decay that only the divine can heal.

Without God imputing His righteousness by faith, our righteousness is as filth rags. In our unredeemed state we cannot work God's miracles because we are foreigners in Zion.

Together, these prophetic signs affirm that God has power over life, nature, and even death. They assured Moses that he carried divine authority, but not in his strength but by God's divine enablement and command. Every miracle worker needs to carry this type of consciousness.

When I am holding a miracle and healing service or crusade anywhere in the world, I close my eyes and then meditate on the glory of God that entered my room many years ago. As soon as I do this, I immediately begin to sense a rising tide of power in my spirit. At times I am so overwhelmed by a divine sense of authority and power that I can almost predict the miracles that will happen! I love operating in the working of miracles!

SYMBOLISM OF SIGNS IN COMMISSIONING

And these signs will follow those who believe: In My name they will cast out demons; they will

> speak with new tongues; they will take up serpents; and if they drink anything deadly, it will by no means hurt them; they will lay hands on the sick, and they will recover (Mark 16:17-18 NKJV).

God doesn't perform these supernatural signs arbitrarily. Each miracle in Moses' call and that of many other servants of God is a symbol. In Moses' case, the burning bush speaks of divine holiness and God's preserving presence. The rod becoming a serpent and returning again illustrates the power of authority and submission. The leprous hand points to Moses' ultimate purification and restoration, as He followed God's call and commandments.

These prophetic signs serve as metaphors for Moses' divine mission. God was letting him know that he will soon confront a serpent-like power in Pharaoh. Interestingly enough, the crowns of all the Pharaohs had a cobra snake in the forefront, illustrating the source of their powers of divination. God was warning Moses in advance not to rely on himself but on what God had placed in his hand. The truth of the matter is that one demon is more powerful than 100 muscled men operating in the power of the flesh. Moses would need purity of heart and divine healing as he led a broken people. *God's signs are not only proofs—they are prophetic images of the journey ahead.*

Every call of God comes with its own arsenal of prophetic or supernatural signs. Every time the great healing evangelist Oral Roberts was in front of a sick person, the power of God would begin to throb in his palms. Not every miracle worker operates like that. It was a sign God specifically gave to brother Roberts. While not always miraculous in the spectacular sense, God confirms His direction through assurance, Scripture, and sometimes visible manifestations. These supernatural signs are not for show—they are for strengthening faith, clarifying purpose, and sealing commitment toward God.

GOD'S POWER DISPLAYED TO VALIDATE HIS CALLING

> So Moses the servant of the Lord died there in the land of Moab, according to the word of the Lord. And He buried him in a valley in the land of Moab, opposite Beth Peor; but no one knows his grave to this day. Moses was one hundred and twenty years old when he died. His eyes were not dim nor his natural vigor diminished. And the children of Israel wept for Moses in the plains of Moab thirty days. So the days of weeping and mourning for Moses ended. Now Joshua the son of Nun was full of the spirit of wisdom, for Moses had laid his hands on him; so the children of Israel heeded him, and did as the Lord had commanded Moses. But since then there has not arisen in Israel a prophet like Moses, whom the Lord knew face to face, in all the signs and wonders which the Lord sent him to do in the land of Egypt, before Pharaoh, before all his servants, and in all his land, and by all that mighty power and all the great terror which Moses performed in the sight of all Israel (Deuteronomy 34:5-12 NKJV).

Ultimately, the miracles in Moses' call serve to validate the divine nature of his assignment. God never calls a man or woman without equipping them with supernatural attestations. He met Moses in fear and uncertainty, not with a harsh rebuke but with a chance at divine revelation. The miraculous signs are God's way of saying, "I will be with you."

Every miracle worker needs this level of divine assurance, because none of us in our humanity can manifest the kind of miracles, signs, and wonders that Moses exhibited in his ministry. There have been several times in my walk of faith when the Holy Spirit overshadowed me with His presence just to assure me that He has called me to be a worker of miracles. Sometimes before I pray for the sick and come against the powers of darkness, I close my eyes, and meditate on these holy moments of divine assurance and then I'm charged up!

God's validation of our calling to the world of miracles is crucial. Moses, a man who once fled Egypt in abject failure, is now being sent back with *dunamis* power. His authority will not rest in his eloquence but in the evidence of God working through him. The rod will part seas and create its own odyssey of miracles. His hands will hold tablets of covenant, written by the finger of God. The fire of God will burn and descend again on Mount Sinai, in the presence of many witnesses. Miracles in the calling of a man or woman are not merely for those who are sent—they are also for those who dare to believe God's words. The Israelites would follow Moses because they saw the miraculous signs. Pharaoh would tremble with fear because he witnessed this awesome power. God's miracles establish the credibility of His messengers.

For modern believers, this chapter reminds us that divine calling is often accompanied by divine confirmation and many miracles. We all may not see burning bushes, but we will encounter moments when God makes His will undeniable. When He calls, He also empowers—and signs follow those who believe according to Mark 16:17-18. Miracles in the call of Moses show that God initiates, equips, and validates those He calls to minister for Him. His presence, His power, and His signs assure the called that they are not alone and neither do they go at it alone. Just as He was with Moses, so He is with us today—still calling, still burning, still working miracles.

Are you ready for your portion of miracles?

LIFE APPLICATION SECTION

Memory Verse

And these signs will follow those who believe: In My name they will cast out demons; they will speak with new tongues; they will take up serpents; and if they drink anything deadly, it will by no means hurt them; they will lay hands on the sick, and they will recover (Mark 16:17-18 NKJV).

Reflections

1. What is the first miracle God showed Moses at the burning bush?

2. What is the second miracle God showed Moses at the burning bush?

____

____

____

____

____

____

____

____

____

____

____

____

PRAYER OF ACTIVATION

Heavenly Father, I bow before You, the God who calls the weak and clothes them with power. As You met Moses in the wilderness, so meet me today. Thank You for the holy fire that burns yet does not consume—the fire of Your presence, the fire of Your holiness, the fire of Your glory. I stand before You now, shoes removed in reverence, yielding my walk, my will, and my ways to Your holy purpose.

Lord Jesus Christ, You are the Captain of my salvation and the Sender of all true messengers. As You called Moses from the flames, so call me out of obscurity into Your marvelous light. Baptize me afresh in

Your fiery presence. Burn away pride, fear, and fleshly ambition. Burn, yet preserve. Burn, yet empower. Let the fire of Your holiness make me a vessel that carries Your miracle-working power to my generation.

Holy Spirit, Spirit of Power and Commission, I yield my heart to Your dealings. Crucify the flesh, silence the carnal mind, and elevate my spirit into heavenly places. Release in me the same glory consciousness that overtook Moses. Dismantle every earthly identity rooted in fear, failure, or past shame. Like Moses' rod, I lay down what is common—my skills, my reputation, my "rod"—and I ask You to transform it for Your glory. What has represented weakness, make it a channel of signs and wonders in my hand.

I renounce the rule of the flesh and the tyranny of the carnal mind.

I embrace consecration, purity, and death to self. Let the fire of God consume every false identity, worldly desire, and demonic influence. Make me spiritually minded, for to be spiritually minded is life and peace. Clothe me with the mantle of heavenly authority. Let my hands be sanctified and healed as You healed Moses' leprous hand, so that my hands may carry the touch of Heaven to the broken and afflicted.

I receive my divine commission as a worker of miracles.

Let signs, wonders, and mighty deeds accompany my obedience as they accompanied Moses. Confirm my calling with Your presence. Fill me with courage to confront the serpent powers of this age not in my strength, but in the demonstration of the Spirit and power. Make my life a living burning bush—ablaze with Your glory yet not consumed. Let all who see know that You have sent me.

Father, as You were with Moses, be with me.

I will not go unless Your presence goes with me. Write Your Word upon my heart as You wrote the covenant on stone. Let the fire that once descended on Sinai rest upon me continually. Let the rod of my life become an instrument that parts seas, brings deliverance, and displays Your glory.

I seal this activation and consecration in the mighty name of Jesus Christ. Amen.

6

RED SEAS, MANNA, AND MIRACULOUS PROVISION

The miracles that accompanied Israel's journey from Egypt to the Promised Land reveal a consistent prophetic pattern: God acts not only out of compassion but in fulfillment of His covenant. Each miraculous act was both a demonstration of divine power and a reinforcement of God's divine relationship with Abraham's seed. From parting seas to daily supernatural provision, from healing through a bronze symbol to judgments turned to mercy, these miracles show that God's miraculous acts are not random—they are intentional, covenantal, and often conditional on obedience to God's word.

> If you are willing and obedient, you shall eat the good of the land (Isaiah 1:19 NKJV).

THE RED SEA CROSSING

> Then Moses stretched out his hand over the sea; and the Lord caused the sea to go back by

a strong east wind all that night, and made the sea into dry land, and the waters were divided. So the children of Israel went into the midst of the sea on the dry ground, and the waters were a wall to them on their right hand and on their left. And the Egyptians pursued and went after them into the midst of the sea, all Pharaoh's horses, his chariots, and his horsemen. Now it came to pass, in the morning watch, that the Lord looked down upon the army of the Egyptians through the pillar of fire and cloud, and He troubled the army of the Egyptians. And He took off their chariot wheels, so that they drove them with difficulty; and the Egyptians said, "Let us flee from the face of Israel, for the Lord fights for them against the Egyptians." Then the Lord said to Moses, "Stretch out your hand over the sea, that the waters may come back upon the Egyptians, on their chariots, and on their horsemen." And Moses stretched out his hand over the sea; and when the morning appeared, the sea returned to its full depth, while the Egyptians were fleeing into it. So the Lord overthrew the Egyptians in the midst of the sea. Then the waters returned and covered the chariots, the horsemen, and all the army of Pharaoh that came into the sea after them. Not so much as one of them remained. But the children of Israel had walked on dry land in the midst of the sea, and the waters were a wall to them on their right hand and on their left. So the Lord saved Israel that day out of the hand of the Egyptians, and Israel saw the Egyptians dead on the seashore. Thus Israel saw the great work which the Lord had done in Egypt; so the people feared

> the Lord, and believed the Lord and His servant Moses (Exodus 14:21-31 NKJV).

In Exodus 14:21-31, Israel faces an impossible situation: an impassable Red Sea flowing in front of them, between them and their land of promise, while simultaneously knowing that Pharaoh's mighty army was marching ferociously toward them from behind.

God instructed Moses to stretch out his rod toward the Red Sea. Immediately the sea parted by the influence of a God-given strong east wind, creating dry ground on which the children of Israel could cross. Once they passed through the parted Red Sea, the waters returned immediately to their original levels in full force and destroyed the entire Egyptian army. This moment of divine intervention becomes the defining act of deliverance in Israel's history. An act of God still talked about to this very day and even immortalized in Hollywood movies.

The Red Sea miracle demonstrates that God is not merely a Liberator from slavery but a Protector against future oppression. It reveals His absolute authority over nature and His unwavering commitment to those in covenant with Him. The Red Sea crossing is not just an escape from tyranny—it was the burial of bondage and the opening of a new identity and chapter in the lives of the children of Israel.

Anyone who wishes to be proficient in the working of miracles must appreciate this immutable fact. God will use new miracle workers for exactly the same reason He used Moses for in the lives of the children of Israel—God used Moses to fulfill His covenant and deliver His people from the clutches of the enemy.

HEAVENLY BREAD

And when the layer of dew lifted, there, on the surface of the wilderness, was a small round substance, as fine as frost on the ground. So when the children of Israel saw it, they said to one another, "What is it?" For they did not know what it was. And Moses said to them, "This is the bread which the Lord has given you to eat. This is the thing which the Lord has commanded: 'Let every man gather it according to each one's need, one omer for each person, according to the number of persons; let every man take for those who are in his tent.'"

Then the children of Israel did so and gathered, some more, some less. So when they measured it by omers, he who gathered much had nothing left over, and he who gathered little had no lack. Every man had gathered according to each one's need. And Moses said, "Let no one leave any of it till morning." Notwithstanding they did not heed Moses. But some of them left part of it until morning, and it bred worms and stank. And Moses was angry with them. So they gathered it every morning, every man according to his need. And when the sun became hot, it melted.

And so it was, on the sixth day, that they gathered twice as much bread, two omers for each one. And all the rulers of the congregation came and told Moses. Then he said to them, "This is what the Lord has said: 'Tomorrow is a Sabbath rest, a holy Sabbath to the Lord. Bake what you will bake today, and boil what you will boil; and lay up for yourselves all that remains, to be kept until morning.'" So they laid it up till morning,

> as Moses commanded; and it did not stink, nor were there any worms in it. Then Moses said, "Eat that today, for today is a Sabbath to the Lord; today you will not find it in the field. Six days you shall gather it, but on the seventh day, the Sabbath, there will be none." Now it happened that some of the people went out on the seventh day to gather, but they found none. And the Lord said to Moses, "How long do you refuse to keep My commandments and My laws? See! For the Lord has given you the Sabbath; therefore He gives you on the sixth day bread for two days. Let every man remain in his place; let no man go out of his place on the seventh day." So the people rested on the seventh day. And the house of Israel called its name Manna. And it was like white coriander seed, and the taste of it was like wafers made with honey.
>
> Then Moses said, "This is the thing which the Lord has commanded: 'Fill an omer with it, to be kept for your generations, that they may see the bread with which I fed you in the wilderness, when I brought you out of the land of Egypt.'" And Moses said to Aaron, "Take a pot and put an omer of manna in it, and lay it up before the Lord, to be kept for your generations." As the Lord commanded Moses, so Aaron laid it up before the Testimony, to be kept. And the children of Israel ate manna forty years, until they came to an inhabited land; they ate manna until they came to the border of the land of Canaan (Exodus 16:14-35 NKJV).

Soon after, in Exodus 16:14-35, the people grumbled about hunger in the wilderness. God answered them supernaturally with manna— "bread from

Heaven" that appeared each morning. It was daily, sufficient, and ceased on the Sabbath as a test of the people's trust in God. Manna was not only supernatural provision—it was a discipline in the school of obedience. Gathering more than needed resulted in the manna rotting. Keeping it on the Sabbath honored God's rhythm that He set in the rhythm of creation.

These two miracles together show God's desire to not only save His people but also to sustain them. Every act of divine deliverance is followed by daily dependence on God. The same God who opens seas also feeds His people through the dew from Heaven. There is no end to the realm of possibilities when we walk in the working of miracles!

THE BRONZE SERPENT LIFTED FOR HEALING

> And the people spoke against God and against Moses: "Why have you brought us up out of Egypt to die in the wilderness? For there is no food and no water, and our soul loathes this worthless bread." So the Lord sent fiery serpents among the people, and they bit the people; and many of the people of Israel died. Therefore the people came to Moses, and said, "We have sinned, for we have spoken against the Lord and against you; pray to the Lord that He take away the serpents from us." So Moses prayed for the people. Then the Lord said to Moses, "Make a fiery serpent, and set it on a pole; and it shall be that everyone who is bitten, when he looks at it,

> shall live." So Moses made a bronze serpent, and put it on a pole; and so it was, if a serpent had bitten anyone, when he looked at the bronze serpent, he lived (Numbers 21:5-9 NKJV).

In Numbers 21:5-9, the Israelites began to complain and murmur again, this time against both God and Moses. In response, God sent fiery serpents as harbingers of divine judgment. Many were bitten by these serpents and died. However, when the people repented for the sin of murmuring and complaining, God instructed Moses to make a bronze serpent and lift it on a pole. Those who looked at it were healed. Jesus would later use this story in the New Testament to point to His death on the Cross and signified that whoever looks to Him for salvation will be delivered from the poison of that old serpent, satan.

This miracle was a manifestation of both judgment and mercy. The bronze serpent did not prevent the bite—it provided healing from it. It symbolized Jesus' substitutionary work and our faith in His finished work of redemption. The people of Israel had to look—an act of trust and acknowledgment of their need for salvation. Jesus later references this moment in John 3:14 (ESV) saying, *"As Moses lifted up the serpent in the wilderness, so must the Son of Man be lifted up."* The bronze serpent foreshadows the Cross of Calvary. Healing flows not from avoidance of sin but from gazing in faith at the One who became sin for us (2 Corinthians 5:21). This miracle also reinforces the principle that God heals on His terms—not ours. The people had to obey the strange divine instruction to receive restoration.

GOD AS DELIVERER, PROVIDER, AND HEALER

The miracles of the wilderness portray God in three vital roles (areas He still operates in today):

1. **Deliverer** – At the Red Sea, God rescued His people from what they could not escape by human means. God intervenes in moments of helplessness and defends us against overwhelming enemies.
2. **Provider** – In the provision of the manna from Heaven, God fed, sustained, and disciplined His people. He doesn't just give what is needed, He teaches us to trust Him through His supernatural provision.
3. **Healer** – Through the bronze serpent, God restored what had been broken by His people's disobedience. Healing comes through repentance and faith.

These divine roles are not isolated acts—they are consistent expressions of God's covenant identity. He promised to be all these things to Israel (Exodus 15:26), and He proved it through supplying miracles. Each intervention was not only an act of compassion for His people but a reinforcement of His divine promises. His promises in Christ Jesus are "yes and amen." For today's believer, these aspects of God remain. He delivers from sin, provides spiritual and material needs, and heals hearts, bodies, and relationships. The wilderness miracles are not just history—they are testimonies to miracles God intends to repeat.

MIRACLES AS COVENANTAL PROVISION AND OBEDIENCE

One of the most striking lessons from these stories is that miracles are tied to covenantal obedience. God's power is always available, but its manifestation often depends on our response. Moses had to stretch his rod. The people had to collect manna correctly. The sick had to look at the bronze serpent. This does not mean God's love is earned. None of us can work hard enough to qualify for God's *agape* love. It means His power flows in the context of relationship. Obedience opens the channel of the miraculous. God was teaching Israel that miracles are not merely moments of rescue—they are tools of formation. Through them, He revealed His divine nature and shaped theirs.

Even Jesus, when performing miracles, often required faith or obedience: *"Stretch out your hand," "Go wash in the pool," "Only believe."* Miracles follow faith-filled action. Covenant is not passive—it is participatory and requires appropriation on our end. God's covenant still operates today through Christ (Messiah). We are His people, and He remains the same Deliverer, Provider, and Healer. But we must walk in trust, obedience, and faith to fully experience the miraculous provisions of the covenant.

The Red Sea, the manna, and the bronze serpent all point to a bigger story: God with His people, working wonders, calling for faith, and shaping them into a holy nation. Miracles in the wilderness weren't just survival tactics—they were covenantal expressions of the God who walks with His own.

LIFE APPLICATION SECTION

MEMORY VERSE

And the people spoke against God and against Moses: "Why have you brought us up out of Egypt to die in the wilderness? For there is no food and no water, and our soul loathes this worthless bread." So the Lord sent fiery serpents among the people, and they bit the people; and many of the people of Israel died. Therefore the people came to Moses, and said, "We have sinned, for we have spoken against the Lord and against you; pray to the Lord that He take away the serpents from us." So Moses prayed for the people. Then the Lord said to Moses, "Make a fiery serpent, and set it on a pole; and it shall be that everyone who is bitten, when he looks at it, shall live." So Moses made a bronze serpent, and put it on a pole; and so it was, if a serpent had bitten anyone, when he looked at the bronze serpent, he lived (Numbers 21:5-9 NKJV).

REFLECTIONS

1. What did God tell the children of Israel to look at in order to get healed?

____

____

____

____

2. What did Moses do in order to part the Red Sea?

PRAYER OF ACTIVATION

Abba Father, Covenant Keeper, I worship You—the God who parts seas, feeds in the wilderness, and heals the bitten. You act in compassion and in covenant. Your mercy endures forever; Your faithfulness reaches to all generations. As You swore to Abraham and confirmed through Moses, so You remember Your people today.

Lord Jesus Christ, You are the Yes and Amen of every promise, the true Bread from Heaven, the One lifted up like the bronze serpent that all who look may live. By Your blood I stand within the New Covenant. I renounce grumbling, unbelief, and fear, and I cleave to Your Word with obedient faith.

Holy Spirit, Spirit of Power and Order, overshadow me now. Write Your statutes on my heart. Align my steps with Heaven's pattern so that miracles flow within covenant boundaries—clean hands, a yielded will, and a listening heart.

I activate covenant faith for three pathways of the miraculous:

1. DELIVERER—RED SEA BREAKTHROUGH

God of the east wind, stretch out Your hand again! By faith I raise the "rod" You've given me—Your Word, my testimony, and Spirit-led obedience. In Jesus' name I command every pursuing bondage, generational chain, and oppressive decree to drown under Your judgment. Open a dry path where there has been no path, and bring me through with spoils and a new identity. I will not look back; I pass through!

2. PROVIDER—MANNA OF DAILY SUFFICIENCY

Bread of Heaven, feed me till I want no more. Teach me the rhythm of obedience: to gather what You give, not hoard from fear; to rest on Your Sabbath; to trust Your double-portion grace. I reject anxiety, scarcity, and self-reliance. I receive wisdom to steward today's portion and faith to expect tomorrow's. Let unexpected supply appear like dew—precise, timely, and enough for every assignment.

3. HEALER—BRONZE SERPENT MERCY

Merciful Redeemer, I look and live. Where sin's venom has burned—body, mind, or soul—I set my gaze on the crucified and risen Christ. I confess my murmuring and repent of hardness of heart. By Your stripes I am healed. Let the power of the Cross neutralize every poison, break every curse, restore what rebellion has ruined, and release wholeness through my hands to others.

COVENANT DECLARATIONS (ISAIAH 1:19)

- I am willing and obedient; therefore, I eat the good of the land.

- Miracles in my life are *intentional, covenantal,* and *aligned with obedience.*
- The Lord fights for me; I will be still and see His salvation.
- I will gather daily, rest faithfully, and steward generously.
- I will keep my eyes on Jesus and minister healing by His authority.

COMMISSIONING

Father, confirm Your Word with signs following. Mark my life with the cloud by day and fire by night. Make me an instrument of deliverance to the trapped, provision to the needy, and healing to the afflicted. Let people see Your great work and fear the Lord, believing You and the servants You send.

I seal this activation in the name of the Father, and of the Son, and of the Holy Spirit. Amen.

7

DIVINE AUTHORITY OVER NATURE AND TIME

Among the most astonishing miracles in Scripture are those in which God alters the fabric of time itself. Time, as a created dimension, is subject to its Creator. In two incredible events—the sun and moon standing still for Joshua and the shadow retreating on Ahaz's sundial in response to Hezekiah's prayer—we see clear evidence that God not only exists outside of time but can intervene within it to fulfill His divine purposes.

These are not poetic metaphors or cosmic coincidences. They are specific interventions by the sovereign God who orchestrates history. Such miracles stretch our understanding of reality, yet they are fully consistent with a theology that recognizes God as Lord over all creation—including time and the heavens.

SUN AND MOON STANDING STILL

> Then Joshua spoke to the Lord in the day when the Lord delivered up the Amorites before the

> children of Israel, and he said in the sight of Israel: "Sun, stand still over Gibeon; and Moon, in the Valley of Aijalon." So the sun stood still, and the moon stopped, till the people had revenge upon their enemies. Is this not written in the Book of Jasher? So the sun stood still in the midst of heaven, and did not hasten to go down for about a whole day. And there has been no day like that, before it or after it, that the Lord heeded the voice of a man; for the Lord fought for Israel (Joshua 10:12-14 NKJV).

In Joshua 10, Israel is fighting a coalition of Amorite kings. As the battle turns in their favor, Joshua prays a bold and unprecedented prayer: *"Sun, stand still over Gibeon; and moon, in the Valley of Aijalon."* And Scripture records that the sun stood still, and the moon stopped, until the nation had avenged its enemies. This miracle is one of cosmic magnitude and demonstrates that humans were given dominion over the elements of nature. In this story, time appears to pause—allowing the Israelites more daylight to secure victory. Verse 14 declares, *"There has been no day like it before or since, that the Lord heeded the voice of a man, for the Lord fought for Israel."*

The miracle that God used Joshua to perform reveals several key truths:

- *God responds to bold faith.* Joshua's prayer was specific and daring.
- *God intervenes in creation for covenant purposes.* The battle was tied to Israel's destiny.
- *God can suspend natural laws for divine timing.* Time bends to God's will when the outcome aligns with His redemptive plan.

This event also emphasizes that miracles serve a purpose beyond wonder. They accomplish strategic objectives in God's Kingdom agenda. In this case, the miracle was not just to prolong the day—it was to ensure total victory and fulfill God's promise to give Israel the land. This realm of the working of miracles is highly unlikely because the reason for stopping the sun and moon would require a highly compelling reason within the redemptive plan of God, notwithstanding our human desire to test the boundaries of the authority we have in Christ.

GOD USES ME TO CALL DOWN RAIN

In 2024, I was ministering in the Republic of Zambia, when I a received a phone call from the vice president's office. She told me that the government had organized a day of "Prayer for the Rain," and the President, Hakainde Hichilema, and his entire cabinet and members of the military would be in attendance. She specifically asked me to pray for rain on national television during the event. The nation of Zambia had suffered a very severe drought the year previously and could not afford a second one. All weather indicators were pointing to another devastating drought.

Everyone was very concerned because the previous drought created power supply failures, electricity load sharing and rationing, and many farming projects failed. I had just written a book on *Mobilizing the Four Winds,* so I knew that the North wind is the one that carries rain; I was fully prepared for my assignment.

When I was finally called to the podium to pray in front of our republic president and thousands of Christians from all walks of life, I immediately went into my prepared speech and prayer. I took the nation into the Courts of Heaven to repent over national sins that were giving satan a legal foothold over the climate of the nation.

I quoted Proverbs 25:23 (NKJV), which says, *"The north wind brings forth rain, and a backbiting tongue an angry countenance."* Then I proceeded to call the North wind to begin to blow over the nation of Zambia and bring forth rain. In less than an hour after my prayer, it started raining. It rained for many months even causing floods in certain areas. The much anticipated national drought did not materialize. This is another realm of the working of miracles.

SHADOW GOES BACKWARD ON AHAZ'S SUNDIAL

> Then Isaiah said, "This is the sign to you from the Lord, that the Lord will do the thing which He has spoken: shall the shadow go forward ten degrees or go backward ten degrees?" And Hezekiah answered, "It is an easy thing for the shadow to go down ten degrees; no, but let the shadow go backward ten degrees." So Isaiah the prophet cried out to the Lord, and He brought the shadow ten degrees backward, by which it had gone down on the sundial of Ahaz (2 Kings 20:9-11 NKJV).

In 2 Kings 20, King Hezekiah is severely sick and is told by the prophet Isaiah that his death was imminent. In a moment of holy desperation, he cried and prayed to God, reminding God of all his works of righteousness. God heard his cry and granted him 15 more years of life. As confirmation of this divine promise, God offers him a miraculous sign.

The prophet Isaiah tells Hezekiah to choose whether the shadow should move forward or backward on the sundial of Ahaz. Hezekiah chooses the harder sign—the shadow going backward. He knew this latter sign would require an absolute miracle, as the sign involved turning back the laws of nature.

The prophet Isaiah prayed, and God caused the shadow to reverse by ten steps (degrees). This miracle was deeply symbolic. The shadow, a divine marker of time, is reversed as a sign of his life being supernaturally extended. God does not merely pause time—He reverses its visible effects, so there was cataclysmic disturbance in the natural flow of things. This miraculous act shows that God is not only the Author of time but the One who governs its progression and very existence.

To humans, time is linear and irreversible. But to God, it is flexible and bendable. God by the working of miracles through a yielded vessel stepped into the timeline of history and adjusted it to align with His covenant and compassion for His people.

Hezekiah's miracle shows that God's promises are not limited by chronological constraints. When He decrees restoration or extension, time will submit to Him. The miracle also underscored the fact that bending time is part of humankind's dominion mandate, if he does it expressly for the will of God!

TIME SUSPENDED FOR DIVINE PURPOSE

In both Joshua's and Hezekiah's experiences, the divine manipulation of time served specific divine purposes:

- *For Joshua:* To ensure military victory and fulfill the promise of Israel possessing the land that God gave to Abraham by covenant.
- *For Hezekiah:* To confirm his divine healing and extend his life in response to faith and prayer.

These are not random displays of divine power—they are calculated actions in line with God's redemptive narrative and nature. God is never wasteful in the miraculous and those believing God to use them in the working of miracles cannot afford to be wasteful or be driven by mere human ambition. When time is suspended or reversed, it is because divine destiny demands it and the resulting miracle will anchor God's will and purpose.

These miracles also encourage us to believe that time is not our enemy when God is our ally. Delays, limitations, and looming deadlines do not limit His sovereignty. If necessary, God will adjust time itself to keep His word. This commit to His spoken words is the primary reason God works miracles.

GOD'S SUPREMACY OVER CHRONOLOGY AND COSMIC FORCES

The manipulation of the sun, moon, and shadow reveals God's supremacy over the cosmos. Ancient cultures worshipped celestial bodies, believing them to control fate. Yet Scripture presents the God who commands the heavens. According to Job 38:33, we can learn the ordinances (laws) of these heavenly bodies and gadgets and use them to establish our dominion over earthly affairs for God's glory.

In Genesis, God created the sun and moon to govern times and seasons. In Joshua, He divinely halts their movement. In 2 Kings, God altered their visible patterns. Time and space are not autonomous—they are instruments in God's hand. This makes them fall within the territory of worker of miracles who are Heaven-bent on demonstrating the power of God to their generation.

This truth is foundational for faith and the working of miracles. God is not bound by time, gravity, or cosmic order. He is the One who set them in place and then placed them under mankind's dominion. As such, He can intervene, override, or redirect them according to His will. This also underscores why "true dominion" even though mandated to man, is not possible at high levels of the miraculous without totally yielding to the power and Person of the Holy Spirit.

For believers who are walking by faith, this truth brings comfort and courage. Delays are not defeats. Deadlines are not destinies. When God purposes a thing, time will accommodate it, one way or the other. This frees us from fear and presses us into a deeper trust in God and His Word.

Because God could suspend the cosmos for Joshua and reverse a shadow for Hezekiah, then He can move Heaven and earth for you, if you dare to believe and be led by the Holy Spirit. *These miracles remind us that we serve the Eternal One—unchanging, all-powerful, and deeply involved in time yet not constrained by it.* In His hands, even time itself becomes a servant to fulfill His divine will and purpose.

LIFE APPLICATION SECTION

Memory Verse

Then Joshua spoke to the Lord in the day when the Lord delivered up the Amorites before the children of Israel, and he said in the sight of Israel: "Sun, stand still over Gibeon; and Moon, in the Valley of Aijalon." So the sun stood still, and the moon stopped, till the people had revenge upon their enemies. Is this not written in the Book of Jasher? So the sun stood still in the midst of heaven, and did not hasten to go down for about a whole day. And there has been no day like that, before it or after it, that the Lord heeded the voice of a man; for the Lord fought for Israel (Joshua 10:12-14 NKJV).

Reflections

1. What did Joshua do to cause the sun to stand still?

____

____

____

____

____

____

____

____

2. What sign did King Hezekiah ask for as evidence that God was going to heal him?

____

____

____

____

____

____

____

____

____

PRAYER OF ACTIVATION

Eternal Father, Ancient of Days, I stand before You, the One who inhabits eternity, who declares the end from the beginning, and who alone holds times and seasons in Your hand. You are not bound by clocks or calendars—time is Your creation, and it bows to Your voice. I exalt You as the Lord of the sun, moon, and stars, the Master of the winds, the Author of my days.

Lord Jesus Christ, Alpha and Omega, You are the same yesterday, today, and forever. In You all things consist. You stopped the sun for Joshua, reversed the shadow for Hezekiah, and in Your mercy extended his life. By Your death and resurrection You shattered the grip of time and mortality. I stand clothed in Your righteousness, washed in Your blood, and joined to Your eternal covenant.

Holy Spirit, Governor of Divine Timings, overshadow me now. Synchronize my life to Heaven's calendar. Baptize me in bold faith like Joshua, holy desperation like Hezekiah, and prophetic precision to discern Heaven's timing. I submit my human deadlines, delays, and detours to Your eternal agenda. Let my spirit rise above earthly clocks into the rhythms of eternity.

By faith I activate this realm of the working of miracles:

1. DOMINION OVER TIME FOR COVENANT FULFILLMENT

In the name of Jesus, I declare: time is not my enemy—it is God's servant. Father, if it will glorify Your name and fulfill Your covenant, suspend time, hasten it, or reverse it for my assignment. Where promises seem late, breathe acceleration. Where my strength seems spent, restore my years like You did for Hezekiah. Redeem wasted seasons and align them to Your redemptive plan.

2. DOMINION OVER COSMIC ORDER FOR KINGDOM VICTORY

As Joshua spoke to the sun and moon, I now speak by delegated authority: let the created order serve the Creator's purpose in my life. I bind the powers that manipulate times and seasons for evil. I decree open heavens, favorable climates, and supernatural extensions of time where needed. Let nature collaborate with Your covenant as I advance Your Kingdom.

3. DOMINION OVER EARTHLY SEASONS BY PROPHETIC DECREES

As I once called forth the North wind and You brought the rains, so I speak to the winds, the seasons, and the elements: align with Heaven's decree. I decree divine timing over every assignment, project, and promise. No drought shall prevail where the Spirit is moving. Let heavenly patterns overwrite demonic forecasts.

COVENANT DECLARATIONS

- I will not fear the ticking clock; my times are in Your hands (Psalm 31:15).
- I walk in preordained works prepared before time began (Ephesians 2:10).
- I am not behind time, I am in God's appointed time.
- Time will not rob me—it will serve me to fulfill the will of God.

COMMISSIONING

Father, confirm this word with signs following. Crown my days with divine encounters, redeem lost years, and compress timelines for Your glory. Let the world know You are God as You work miracles that defy time through this yielded vessel. In Jesus' name, I activate this realm of the miraculous. Amen.

8

FIRE FROM HEAVEN: THE GOD WHO ANSWERS BY FIRE

And fire came out from before the Lord and consumed the burnt offering and the fat on the altar. When all the people saw it, they shouted and fell on their faces (Leviticus 9:24 NKJV).

Elijah has always been my favorite prophet in the Bible. Only God knows how many times I have preached the sermon, "The God Who Answers by Fire!" One of those times, an insane woman bound with over 1,000 demons was miraculously delivered! Throughout Scripture, fire from Heaven is a divine signature—a visible manifestation of God's power and approval. It is God's fingerprint.

In two dramatic moments—Aaron's priestly initiation in Leviticus chapter 9 and Elijah's confrontation with the prophets of Baal on Mount Carmel in 1 Kings 18—God responds to Elijah's sacrifice and prayer with consuming fire. When the fire of God fell, the entire nation of Israel turned toward the Lord. Walking in the consuming fire of the Lord is a critical aspect in the lives of all workers of miracles! The fire falling from Heaven events are not mere displays of supernatural force, they are affirmations of divine covenant, authority, and presence in the life of the believer.

In both cases, the fire from Heaven confirms the legitimacy of God's appointed servants. Fire is how God marks and brands His servants. It also highlights the relationship between consecrated sacrifice, fervent prayer, and the release of God's supernatural power. These altars become not just places of offering, but intersections between Heaven and earth.

FIRE CONSUMES SACRIFICES ON AARON'S AND ELIJAH'S ALTARS

Leviticus 9:24 describes a critical moment in Israel's worship history. After following God's instructions to consecrate the tabernacle and the priesthood of Levi, Aaron offered a burnt offering and peace offering before the people. As the rituals concluded, *"fire came out from before the Lord and consumed the burnt offering.... When all the people saw it, they shouted and fell on their faces."*

This was more than spectacle—it was divine endorsement. God accepted the offering and authenticated the new priesthood. It was His way of saying, "I dwell here; this is My order." The consuming fire declared the sacredness of worship and the seriousness of approaching God on His terms.

No one can operate effectively in the ministry of the working of miracles who does not appreciate the sacredness of divine worship and the utter seriousness of approaching God on His own terms. Doing what God wants is the key to living in the realm of the miraculous. God is not an idol whom we can simply order around. He is the infallible, eternal and self-sufficient One, and relies not on human effort to get His purposes done. It is our greatest privilege to work for Him and through Him!

> Then the fire of the Lord fell and consumed the burnt sacrifice, and the wood and the stones and the dust, and it licked up the water that was in the trench (1 Kings 18:38 NKJV).

In 1 Kings 18:38, the scene shifts to Mount Carmel, where Elijah the prophet confronts the prophets of Baal, who ate at Jezebel's table. He challenged them to prove who was the God who answers by fire, whether Baal or El Elyon! After hours of fruitless, effort-draining, vain rituals by the false prophets, they failed to bring fire from Heaven through the power of satan.

Elijah took over, rebuilt the broken altar of the Lord that had been previously torn down, then prayed a simple, sincere prayer. Then holy fire fell from Heaven and consumed not only the offering on the altar, but the wood, stones, dust, and water in the trench. Upon seeing this supernatural sign, the people fell on their faces and proclaimed, *"The Lord, He is God!"*

This fire served as both divine judgment and revelation. It judged the false priesthood of Jezebel and her prophets, resulting in the public execution of the 450 prophets of Baal. It exposed falsehood and affirmed truth. The fire judged the people's spiritual apathy and set their hearts on fire for God. In this divine moment of national transformation, God responded not to human theatrics but to the living faith and obedience in the heart of Elijah. We must never forget that the working of miracles is for destroying spiritual apathy and turning the heart of a generation back to God.

THE RELATIONSHIP BETWEEN PRAYER, SACRIFICE, AND SUPERNATURAL POWER

Both of these accounts reveal that supernatural fire was not random—it followed specific acts of faith and obedience and alignment with God's will and purpose. In Leviticus, the fire came after detailed obedience to God's command for consecration and sacrifice. In 1 Kings, fire came after a heartfelt prayer rooted in covenant faith and obedience. These spiritual ingredients are necessary in the hearts of all miracle workers who labor in His name.

Fervent and prevailing prayer and sacrifice work together in holy tandem. Sacrifice represents total surrender—giving up what is valuable to us in order to acknowledge God's worth. Prayer is intimate communion with God—reaching out to the divine in total trust and dependence.

Together, these power centers form a spiritual altar, from where miracles, signs, and wonders are birthed. Where there is no altar of surrender, there is neither fire nor power. This is the spiritual cancer behind much of the powerless Christianity we see today!

In Elijah's case, the sacrifice was doused with water, making natural ignition impossible. We will never swim or surrender to the river of God until we give up our dependence on the flesh (mere human effort). Pouring water on the altar emphasized that God's fire is not man-made in any shape or fashion. The fire of God is always as a result of divine response, not mere human manipulation. Likewise, in our lives, the fire of God—His presence, power, and confirmation—comes when our offerings are genuine and our prayers are aligned with His purpose.

These biblical examples teach us that God honors the posture of the heart more than the mechanics of the rituals of the altar. God answers and is drawn to authenticity, not mere human performance.

GOD CONFIRMS HIS SERVANTS WITH VISIBLE POWER

> God also bearing witness both with signs and wonders, with various miracles, and gifts of the Holy Spirit, according to His own will? (Hebrews 2:4 NKJV)

In both narratives, the fire of God served as a divine endorsement of the ministers God was using. For Aaron, it was the beginning of his priestly ministry that would continue for more than 4,000 years. For Elijah, it was the climax of a prophetic confrontation with the Jezebel spirit, which was corrupting the nation of Israel. In both cases, the miraculous fire validated their divine ordination, calling and establishing their spiritual authority before the people.

This principle recurs many times over throughout Scripture. God often confirms His special messengers through visible signs and miraculous demonstrations of power:

- Moses with the burning bush and signs in Egypt.
- Jesus with miracles, healings, and resurrection.
- The apostles with signs following (Mark 16:20).

These divine confirmations are not for the ego of the servant of the Lord but for reviving the faith of God's people. God uses signs and wonders to point to His presence and to affirm the credibility of His Word and messengers.

In the New Testament era, the fire of God may not always be literal, but God still confirms His Word through spiritual fire—hearts burning with conviction, miracles accompanying the gospel, and the power of the Holy Spirit demonstrating that God is with His people. When God answers by fire, it is not only a moment of power—it is a message. It says: God is present. God approves. God reigns.

The fire on Aaron's altar and the fire on Elijah's altar speak across multiple generations. They call us to build lives of worship, sacrifice, and prayer. They remind us of the God who still responds with power wherever He finds absolute surrender and living faith. His holy fire can never be bought or manipulated—it is invited through obedience and holy expectation and consecration.

When we lay our lives on the altar and cry out in faith, Heaven still answers. God's power is not confined to the past. He is the same God who consumes offerings, confirms His servants, and reveals Himself in fire. Let us build our altars with reverence, pray with expectation, and believe for the fire of His presence to fall again.

LIFE APPLICATION SECTION

Memory Verse

And fire came out from before the Lord and consumed the burnt offering and the fat on the altar. When all the people saw it, they shouted and fell on their faces (Leviticus 9:24 NKJV).

Reflections

1. God confirms the word with miracles; what does this mean?

2. What is the relationship between prayer and power?

PRAYER OF ACTIVATION

Most High God, El Elyon, I come before Your throne of grace, clothed in the righteousness of Jesus Christ, washed by His precious blood, and filled with the Holy Spirit. You are the God who dwells in unapproachable light. You are the same God who consumed Aaron's offering with fire, and who sent fire from Heaven to vindicate Your prophet Elijah on Mount Carmel. Today I stand as Your servant, longing to be marked, branded, and consumed by Your holy fire.

Father, I consecrate myself afresh upon the altar of Your will. I renounce the flesh, the carnal mind, and every form of self-dependence. I lay down my gifts, my ambitions, my titles, and my plans as living sacrifices. As Aaron obeyed every divine command and Elijah rebuilt the broken altar, so I rebuild the altar of my heart with repentance, worship, and obedience. Let my life become a resting place for Your glory.

Lord Jesus Christ, High Priest of the New Covenant, I honor the sacrifice You made at Calvary, where the fire of divine judgment fell upon You for my sake. You are the Lamb whose blood speaks a better word. As You rose in power, baptize me with the same Holy Spirit and fire You promised to Your disciples. Let my heart burn with Your passion, my words burn with Your truth, and my hands burn with Your power to heal, deliver, and raise the dead.

Holy Spirit, Fire of the Living God, fall upon me now. Ignite my spirit, soul, and body with holy flames. Burn away compromise, unbelief, pride, and apathy. Brand me as Your vessel. Let the fire of Your presence rest on my life as a visible sign of divine approval, just as You did with Aaron and Elijah. Let Your fire be the seal of Heaven upon the altar of my obedience.

I now activate by faith the realm of the "working of miracles" by fire:

- *Let every altar of prayer I build become a point of divine encounter.*
- *Let my words carry the voltage of Your Spirit, overthrowing idols, false doctrines, and demonic thrones.*
- *Let the fire of God fall wherever I preach, pray, or minister, consuming sickness, destroying yokes, and turning hearts back to You.*

- *Let the fire validate my calling and confirm Your Word with signs, wonders, and miracles following (Hebrews 2:4, Mark 16:20).*

Father, let it be known this day—as it was on Carmel—that You are God in Israel, and that I am Your servant, and that I have done all these things at Your word. Answer by fire, O Lord, and let Your people fall on their faces and proclaim, "The Lord, He is God! The Lord, He is God!"

Consume my life, and let Your fire be seen in my generation.

I receive my mantle of fire and miracle power now, in the mighty name of Jesus Christ. Amen.

9

SIGNS AND WONDERS THROUGH PROPHETIC VESSELS

Here am I and the children whom the Lord has given me! We are for signs and wonders in Israel from the Lord of hosts, who dwells in Mount Zion

(Isaiah 8:18 NKJV).

Miracles, signs, and wonders often do more than meet immediate human needs—they confirm divine election and levels of spiritual authority and reveal enduring dimensions of divine anointment. In the lives of God's prophets, signs frequently served to validate leadership, reinforce divine selection, and display the lingering presence of the Holy Spirit even beyond a prophet's death. From Aaron's rod miraculously budding, to a borrowed axe head floating on a body of water, to a dead man revived by touching Elisha's bones, Scripture reveals that the anointing upon God's servants carries weight far beyond the moment.

These signs and wonders served as divine markers in the journey of the children of Israel, reinforcing the reality that when God places His hand on a vessel, that vessel becomes a conduit of supernatural power and manifestations. True spiritual "authority" is not self-appointed—it is confirmed by divine presence and evidence.

AARON'S BUDDING ROD

> And the Lord spoke to Moses, saying: "Speak to the children of Israel, and get from them a rod from each father's house, all their leaders according to their fathers' houses—twelve rods. Write each man's name on his rod. And you shall write Aaron's name on the rod of Levi. For there shall be one rod for the head of each father's house. Then you shall place them in the tabernacle of meeting before the Testimony, where I meet with you. And it shall be that the rod of the man whom I choose will blossom; thus I will rid Myself of the complaints of the children of Israel, which they make against you." So Moses spoke to the children of Israel, and each of their leaders gave him a rod apiece, for each leader according to their fathers' houses, twelve rods; and the rod of Aaron was among their rods. And Moses placed the rods before the Lord in the tabernacle of witness. Now it came to pass on the next day that Moses went into the tabernacle of witness, and behold, the rod of Aaron, of the house of Levi, had sprouted and put forth buds, had produced blossoms and yielded ripe almonds. Then Moses brought out all the rods from before

> the Lord to all the children of Israel; and they looked, and each man took his rod. And the Lord said to Moses, "Bring Aaron's rod back before the Testimony, to be kept as a sign against the rebels, that you may put their complaints away from Me, lest they die." Thus did Moses; just as the Lord had commanded him, so he did (Numbers 17:1-11, NKJV).

This miracle occurred during a time of leadership crisis. Korah's rebellion in Numbers 16 had challenged the divine appointment of Moses and Aaron. To silence ongoing disputes and prove whom God had chosen as high priest, God instructed each tribal leader to place a rod before the Ark of the Covenant. The rod of the man God chose would blossom. This was a divinely brilliant idea. This was the silver bullet God needed to silence the unnecessary squabbles over titles and leadership.

The next day, Aaron's rod not only sprouted buds—it had bloomed and borne ripe almonds. This was a supernatural act: a dead piece of wood had not only come to life but had completed a full cycle of growth overnight. This is also what I call the quickening anointing!

This miracle had profound meaning:

- It confirmed God's chosen authority.
- It symbolized resurrection power and fruitfulness coming from death.
- It demonstrated that divine calling bears visible, supernatural fruit.

Aaron's rod that budded was placed before the Ark as a testimony, reminding the people that spiritual authority is divinely given, not politically earned. Leadership in the Kingdom is authenticated by the fruit and favor that follow divine commission.

THE FLOATING AXE HEAD

> But as one was cutting down a tree, the iron ax head fell into the water; and he cried out and said, "Alas, master! For it was borrowed." So the man of God said, "Where did it fall?" And he showed him the place. So he cut off a stick, and threw it in there; and he made the iron float. Therefore he said, "Pick it up for yourself." So he reached out his hand and took it (2 Kings 6:5-7 NKJV).

In this brief but powerful account, the prophet Elisha is with a group of prophetic apprentices when one of them loses a borrowed iron axe head in the Jordan River. The man cries out in distress, and Elisha responds by cutting a stick, throwing it into the water, and causing the iron to float. What! This miracle defied the laws of both gravity and floatation and yet happened. I believe that men and women of God who will be used by God in similar fashion will steadily increase, worldwide.

Though seemingly minor compared to more dramatic miracles, this prophetic and miraculous act carries significant meaning:

- It shows God's care for practical, even personal needs.
- It reflects prophetic sensitivity to human burden.

- It demonstrates divine power (dominion) over the natural order (iron does not float on water).

The axe-head miracle reveals that no situation is too small for God's intervention. This is how much He loves His children and people in general. The prophetic anointing does not only operate in massive deliverances but also in everyday challenges, one problem at a time. It illustrates God's attentiveness and readiness to respond through His anointed and consecrated servants.

RESURRECTION VIA ELISHA'S BONES

> So it was, as they were burying a man, that suddenly they spied a band of raiders; and they put the man in the tomb of Elisha; and when the man was let down and touched the bones of Elisha, he revived and stood on his feet (2 Kings 13:21 NKJV).

Perhaps one of the most astonishing accounts in all of Scripture is found in 2 Kings 13:21. A group of Israelites were burying a man (the Bible never mentions his name) when they saw raiders, or bandits, approaching. In desperate haste, they threw the body into Elisha's tomb. They quickly practiced the Scripture, *"Let the dead bury the dead"* (see Luke 9:60). When the corpse touched Elisha's bones, the man came to life and stood up. I am sure at seeing this miracle the invaders, or bandits, must have run for their dear lives. Ha!

This miracle, a foreshadowing of the future resurrection of the saints, occurred after Elisha had died, showcasing the residual power of the prophetic anointing or the glory of God on a man's bones. It reveals, the following:

- The enduring nature of God's anointing.
- That proximity to a vessel of God—even posthumously—can trigger supernatural events.
- That God's Spirit, once imparted, leaves lasting impact.

This miraculous account testifies to the fact that the anointing is not temporal. It lives beyond the moment, beyond the minister, and even beyond death. God honors the vessels He uses and allows their influence to echo even from the corridors of eternity.

THE ONGOING INFLUENCE OF PROPHETIC ANOINTING

These three miracles form a mosaic of how God uses supernatural signs to affirm, preserve, and perpetuate the influence of His servants. From the budding of Aaron's priestly rod to the floating of a lost axe head, to the resurrection power of God resting on dry bones—each event demonstrates that when God places His Spirit and glory upon someone, that anointing reshapes and completely alters their reality, even their DNA.

The prophetic anointing does more than foretell things to come—it confirms God's mighty hand. It ministers to people and nations in crisis, affirms divine selection, and sustains the spiritual legacy of God's servants. In the case of Aaron, it silenced rebellion to his priestly position and established God's order. In the case of Elisha, it extended to needs both small and great, even beyond his life. The prophetic anointing is one of the most important ingredients to the working of miracles.

> And it shall come to pass in the last days, says God, that I will pour out of My Spirit on all flesh; your sons and your daughters shall prophesy, your young men shall see visions, your old men shall dream dreams. And on My menservants and on My maidservants I will pour out My Spirit in those days; and they shall prophesy (Acts 2:17-18 NKJV).

Today, believers are called to walk in the awareness that the same Spirit who empowered the prophets now resides in every Spirit-filled believer (Acts 2:17-18). The prophetic anointing is not locked in the past—it is very much alive in the Church today. While our bones may not raise the dead, our prayers can, and our words can heal and our obedience can bear supernatural fruit.

God still confirms His servants—not by their titles, but by His power flowing through them. The legacy of the prophetic anointing is this: *where there is obedience, humility, and alignment with God's will, there will be signs and wonders that follow.*

These biblical stories remind us that the power of God doesn't fade with space or time. It multiplies generationally through the faithfulness of His yielded vessels. When we steward His anointing and presence well, its influence continues long after we're gone.

PRAYER OF ACTIVATION

Eternal Father, the Lord of Hosts, I come before You in reverence and holy fear, standing on Your Word in Isaiah 8:18, "Here am I and the children whom the Lord has given me! We are for signs and wonders in Israel from the Lord of hosts, who dwells in Mount Zion." Today I present myself and the spiritual sons and daughters You have entrusted to me. We belong to You, and we are ordained to be living vessels of Your signs, wonders, and miracles in our generation.

Lord, I acknowledge that true spiritual authority is not assumed—it is conferred. You confirmed Aaron's priesthood when his rod budded. You authenticated Elisha's prophetic office when a borrowed axe head floated, and You displayed the enduring residue of Your glory when a dead man revived by touching Elisha's bones. These holy signs were not human inventions, they were divine endorsements. Father, I renounce every carnal ambition, pride, and striving for positions. I choose humility, consecration, and total obedience as the only acceptable posture for carrying Your prophetic anointing.

Lord Jesus Christ, Anointed One, and Chief Cornerstone, You are the embodiment of the prophetic Spirit. You declared that the Spirit of the Lord is upon You to heal, deliver, and proclaim the acceptable year of the Lord. Now as Your co-laborer, I ask: Let the same Spirit that rested on the prophets rest on me. Let resurrection life flow from my words, healing flow from my hands, and divine solutions spring forth from my lips. May Your living anointing dismantle rebellion, silence confusion, and establish Your order wherever I am sent.

Holy Spirit, Spirit of Prophecy and Power, breathe upon me afresh. Let Your prophetic fire saturate my spirit, soul, and body. Let the mantle of prophetic authority rest on me, confirmed by signs, wonders, and miracles that glorify Jesus alone. I decree that everything dead around me will bud like Aaron's rod, everything lost will surface like the floating axe head, and everything hopeless will rise to life by the resurrection power that once flowed through Elisha's bones. Let the prophetic anointing in me outlive me and bless generations yet unborn.

Father, I boldly activate by faith this realm of the working of miracles:

- *I declare that I and the children You have given me are for signs and wonders.*
- *I decree that Your power will confirm my assignment, silence rebellion, and establish divine order.*
- *I declare that prophetic solutions will flow from me to meet practical needs and impossible situations.*
- *I decree that Your anointing on my life will not be temporary but generational, enduring beyond my days on earth.*

Lord of Hosts, confirm Your Word in my mouth with signs following (Mark 16:20). Let Your glory rest visibly upon my life as Your testimony. May Your power flowing through me authenticate Your call on my life before others. Father, mark me, brand me, and release me as a living sign to this generation—for Your glory alone.

I receive the prophetic mantle for signs, wonders, and the working of miracles, in Jesus' mighty name. Amen.

10

MIRACLES OF HEALING AND RESTORATION

Then Peter said, "Silver and gold I do not have, but what I do have I give you: In the name of Jesus Christ of Nazareth, rise up and walk." And he took him by the right hand and lifted him up, and immediately his feet and ankle bones received strength. So he, leaping up, stood and walked and entered the temple with them—walking, leaping, and praising God. And all the people saw him walking and praising God. Then they knew that it was he who sat begging alms at the Beautiful Gate of the temple; and they were filled with wonder and amazement at what had happened to him

(Acts 3:6-10 NKJV).

Throughout Scripture, healing is a recurring manifestation of God's power, driven by His compassion and often activated by the faith and obedience of either His servants or the recipients of a miracle. Whether it's the cleansing of a leper, the raising of the paralyzed, or the resurrection of the dead, each miracle reveals something about God's heart and how He interacts with human faith. In the stories of Naaman, the paralytic, and Lazarus, we encounter healing in different forms—physical, relational, and even post-mortem. Yet all share common threads: the mercy of God, the necessity of obedience, and the breakthrough that follows faith. All workers of miracles must respect this divine balance and common thread.

NAAMAN'S HEALING

> And Elisha sent a messenger to him, saying, "Go and wash in the Jordan seven times, and your flesh shall be restored to you, and you shall be clean." But Naaman became furious, and went away and said, "Indeed, I said to myself, 'He will surely come out to me, and stand and call on the name of the Lord his God, and wave his hand over the place, and heal the leprosy.' Are not the Abanah and the Pharpar, the rivers of Damascus, better than all the waters of Israel? Could I not wash in them and be clean?" So he turned and went away in a rage. And his servants came near and spoke to him, and said, "My father, if the prophet had told you to do something great, would you not have done it? How much more then, when he says to you, 'Wash, and be clean'?" So he went down and dipped seven times in the Jordan, according to the saying of the man of God; and his flesh was restored like the flesh of a little child, and he was clean (2 Kings 5:10-14 NKJV).

The healing of Naaman has never ceased to amaze me. It's loaded with just the right tension between the fallacy of pride and the miracle of faith. For many people, pride is the price they pay for not walking in miracles. They choose pride instead of walking humbly before God. Naaman was a commander of the Syrian army—a man of great influence, but he was also a leper. His healing begins not with a dramatic miracle but with a seemingly humiliating instruction: to dip seven times in the Jordan River. Elisha the prophet refused to meet with him personally, but instead he sent a message through his servant Gehazi, telling him what to do.

Initially, Naaman was very offended. He expected spectacle and royal pomp when his chariots arrived. He wanted honor and ceremony. He was used to such treatment in Syria. Instead, he is asked to obey a simple but unglamorous command. It is only after his servants persuaded him to humble himself and do as instructed that Naaman obeys. As he dips in the Jordan River seven times, his leprous skin is restored like that of a young child.

Naaman's story teaches us that healing often comes through obedience, even when the instruction feels beneath us. God resists pride but responds to humility. Miracles are not earned—they are received by submission to God's will and method. This account also reveals the inclusivity of God's compassion. Naaman was not an Israelite, yet God healed him. It foreshadows the New Testament expansion of grace to the Gentiles and affirms that faith, not pedigree, accesses divine healing.

PARALYTIC LOWERED THROUGH THE ROOF

And again He entered Capernaum after some days, and it was heard that He was in the house. Immediately many gathered together, so that there was no longer room to receive them, not even near the door. And He preached the word to them. Then they came to Him, bringing a paralytic who was carried by four men. And when they could not come near Him because of the crowd, they uncovered the roof where He was. So when they had broken through, they let down the bed on which the paralytic was lying. When Jesus saw their faith, He said to the paralytic, "Son, your sins are forgiven you." And some of the scribes were sitting there and reasoning in their hearts, "Why does this Man speak blasphemies like this? Who can forgive sins but God alone?" But immediately, when Jesus perceived in His spirit that they reasoned thus within themselves, He said to them, "Why do you reason about these things in your hearts? Which is easier, to say to the paralytic, 'Your sins are forgiven you,' or to say, 'Arise, take up your bed and walk'? But that you may know that the Son of Man has power on earth to forgive sins"—He said to the paralytic, "I say to you, arise, take up your bed, and go to your house." Immediately he arose, took up the bed, and went out in the presence of them all, so that all were amazed and glorified God, saying, "We never saw anything like this!" (Mark 2:1-12 NKJV)

In Mark chapter 2, a paralyzed man is brought to Jesus by friends who cannot access the house due to the crowd. Undeterred, they tear open the roof and lower him down. This is what I call aggressive faith. Jesus sees their faith—not just the man's, but his friends'—and says, "Son, your sins are forgiven." This declaration shocks the religious leaders (the Pharisees and the Sadducees), but Jesus then confirms His authority by healing the man physically, saying, *"Rise, take up your mat, and walk."*

This moment reveals the multidimensional nature of healing. Jesus addresses the man's deeper need—forgiveness of sin—before healing his body. Healing is holistic in the Kingdom of God. It encompasses spirit, soul, and body. Faith plays a central role. It was faith that tore open the roof. Faith that refused to be blocked by obstacles. Faith that partnered with compassion. The man obeys Jesus' command to rise—and is instantly made whole.

This account encourages persistent, action-oriented faith. It also highlights the role of community. Sometimes, healing comes not only through personal belief but through the faith of others on our behalf. I am a strong believer in the working of miracles through the corporate anointing.

LAZARUS RAISED FROM THE DEAD

Jesus said to her, "I am the resurrection and the life. He who believes in Me, though he may die, he shall live. And whoever lives and believes in

Me shall never die. Do you believe this?" She said to Him, "Yes, Lord, I believe that You are the Christ, the Son of God, who is to come into the world." And when she had said these things, she went her way and secretly called Mary her sister, saying, "The Teacher has come and is calling for you." As soon as she heard that, she arose quickly and came to Him. Now Jesus had not yet come into the town, but was in the place where Martha met Him. Then the Jews who were with her in the house, and comforting her, when they saw that Mary rose up quickly and went out, followed her, saying, "She is going to the tomb to weep there." Then, when Mary came where Jesus was, and saw Him, she fell down at His feet, saying to Him, "Lord, if You had been here, my brother would not have died." Therefore, when Jesus saw her weeping, and the Jews who came with her weeping, He groaned in the spirit and was troubled. And He said, "Where have you laid him?" They said to Him, "Lord, come and see." Jesus wept. Then the Jews said, "See how He loved him!" And some of them said, "Could not this Man, who opened the eyes of the blind, also have kept this man from dying?" Then Jesus, again groaning in Himself, came to the tomb. It was a cave, and a stone lay against it. Jesus said, "Take away the stone." Martha, the sister of him who was dead, said to Him, "Lord, by this time there is a stench, for he has been dead four days." Jesus said to her, "Did I not say to you that if you would believe you would see the glory of God?" Then they took away the stone from the place where the dead man was lying. And Jesus lifted up His eyes and said, "Father, I thank You that You have heard Me. And I

> know that You always hear Me, but because of the people who are standing by I said this, that they may believe that You sent Me." Now when He had said these things, He cried with a loud voice, "Lazarus, come forth!" And he who had died came out bound hand and foot with grave-clothes, and his face was wrapped with a cloth. Jesus said to them, "Loose him, and let him go" (John 11:25-44 NKJV).

The story of Lazarus is the pinnacle of Christ's healing ministry before the Cross. There was no greater miracle than the healing of Lazarus, outside of being born again. Lazarus was not just sick—he was dead and buried. Jesus delays His arrival, allowing the situation to reach its darkest point. When He arrives, Martha voices a familiar blend of faith and sorrow: *"If you had been here, my brother would not have died."* Martha's response underscores the spiritual cancer of warped faith that sounds like faith but is not. Martha's faith was both past tense and future tense but not *now! "If You had been here* [past tense] *my brother would not have died."* This is not Bible faith, and it does not lend itself to the working of miracles.

Jesus responds with one of the most profound declarations in Scripture: *"I am the resurrection and the life."* He then weeps—showing His deep compassion—and proceeds to call forth Lazarus from the grave. With a loud voice, Jesus commands, *"Lazarus, come out!"* The man who had been dead four days walked out of the tomb, wrapped in grave clothes.

This miracle shows that even death is not beyond the reach of Jesus. It reveals His divine identity and the fullness of His authority. But it also shows the emotional depth of God's heart. Jesus was not distant or detached—He was moved.

Obedience is also present. The stone had to be rolled away. The people had to participate in removing the grave clothes. Even in miracles, God often includes human partnership. This is a very important lesson for all workers of miracles.

FAITH, OBEDIENCE, AND THE COMPASSION OF GOD IN HEALING

These three stories—Naaman, the paralytic, and Lazarus—offer a complete picture of how healing operates in God's economy of glory:

- *Faith* moves people to act. It climbs roofs, dips in rivers, and believes despite death.
- *Obedience* activates divine intervention. God honors those who follow His instructions, even when they seem illogical.
- *Compassion* motivates the miracle. Jesus' heart breaks for the broken. He heals not just to prove His power, but to restore human dignity, relationship, and life.

Healing is never merely functional in Scripture—it is relational. God heals to reveal Himself, to draw people closer, and to manifest His Kingdom. Workers of miracles must do their best to be relational in their ministry.

In a world still filled with pain and sickness, these accounts offer enduring hope. God still heals. He still responds to faith. He still honors obedience. And most of all, He still feels compassion. Whether we are like Naaman in need of humility, the paralytic dependent on others, or Lazarus seemingly beyond hope—God's healing touch is available. He is the God who cleanses, restores, and resurrects. And His miracles are as much about revealing His nature as they are about removing our afflictions.

LIFE APPLICATION SECTION

MEMORY VERSE

Then Peter said, "Silver and gold I do not have, but what I do have I give you: In the name of Jesus Christ of Nazareth, rise up and walk." And he took him by the right hand and lifted him up, and immediately his feet and ankle bones received strength. So he, leaping up, stood and walked and entered the temple with them—walking, leaping, and praising God. And all the people saw him walking and praising God. Then they knew that it was he who sat begging alms at the Beautiful Gate of the temple; and they were filled with wonder and amazement at what had happened to him (Acts 3:6-10 NKJV).

REFLECTIONS

1. What is the first miracle Peter and John worked after Pentecost?

____

____

____

____

____

____

____

2. How many days was Lazarus in the tomb?

PRAYER OF ACTIVATION

Righteous Father, the God of Mercy and Healing, I come boldly to Your throne of grace through the blood of Jesus, standing on Acts 3:6-10 where Peter declared, "Silver and gold I do not have, but what I do have I give you: In the name of Jesus Christ of Nazareth, rise up and walk." Lord, today I receive and activate this same mantle of miracle-working power—not to exalt myself, but to magnify the name of Jesus and to bring restoration to the broken, the sick, and the afflicted.

Lord Jesus Christ, my Great Physician and Resurrection Life, You cleansed the leper, raised the paralyzed, and called the dead back to life. You touched Naaman's pride and healed his flesh. You honored the faith of friends and raised a paralytic from his mat. You wept with Mary and Martha, then commanded Lazarus to come forth. You are the same yesterday, today, and forever. I proclaim that Your healing virtue flows through me because Your Spirit lives in me. As You were moved with compassion then, move through me now to heal the sick, cleanse the oppressed, and restore the brokenhearted.

Holy Spirit, Breath of Life and Divine Power, I yield fully to You. Clothe me with Your anointing to heal, restore, and resurrect. Empower me to speak words that carry Your life, to lay hands that transmit Your power, and to love with Your compassion. Remove pride from me, and fill me with humility and quick obedience to Your voice, even when Your instructions defy logic. Make me sensitive to the corporate faith of the body of Christ, and help me partner with others in releasing Your healing presence.

By faith, I now activate this dimension of the working of miracles:

- *I declare that faith will rise in me and through me to act boldly in Your name.*
- *I decree that obedience will align me with divine instructions that open the door to miracles.*
- *I declare that the compassion of Christ will flow from my heart, releasing healing, deliverance, and restoration to all who are bound or broken.*
- *I decree that resurrection power will manifest, raising to life what has died and restoring what has been lost or stolen.*

Father, in Jesus' mighty name, I call forth creative miracles, instantaneous healings, and supernatural restorations. I command spiritual paralysis to break, emotional leprosy to be cleansed, and every spiritual grave to open. I speak to dry bones: live again. I speak to diseased bodies: be made whole. I speak to shattered hearts: be restored. I speak to dormant destinies: awaken now by the power of the Holy Spirit!

Lord, confirm Your Word through my life with signs, wonders, and healings that draw souls to Jesus. Make me a vessel of mercy, a carrier of Your glory, and a channel of Your healing river.

I receive by faith this mantle for miracles of healing and restoration—in the mighty name of Jesus Christ. Amen.

11

THE APOSTOLIC MIRACLES: OUR AUTHORITY IN CHRIST'S NAME

And through the hands of the apostles many signs and wonders were done among the people. And they were all with one accord in Solomon's Porch
(Acts 5:12 NKJV).

The book of Acts reveals that the miraculous did not end with Jesus' ascension. Rather, His power and authority continued—and even expanded—through the Church. In three remarkable stories, we see apostles exercising divine authority: Peter and John heal a lame man; Paul blinds a sorcerer; and handkerchiefs carry healing from Paul's body. These events demonstrate that miracles were not limited to Christ's earthly ministry but were passed on as part of the Church's mission.

These miracles not only validated the apostles' message but also illustrated the new dynamic at work: the Holy Spirit indwelling believers, empowering them to be vessels of divine intervention. The

Church was—and remains—a living extension of Christ's authority on earth.

PETER AND JOHN HEALING THE LAME MAN

> Now Peter and John went up together to the temple at the hour of prayer, the ninth hour. And a certain man lame from his mother's womb was carried, whom they laid daily at the gate of the temple which is called Beautiful, to ask alms from those who entered the temple; who, seeing Peter and John about to go into the temple, asked for alms. And fixing his eyes on him, with John, Peter said, "Look at us." So he gave them his attention, expecting to receive something from them. Then Peter said, "Silver and gold I do not have, but what I do have I give you: In the name of Jesus Christ of Nazareth, rise up and walk." And he took him by the right hand and lifted him up, and immediately his feet and ankle bones received strength. So he, leaping up, stood and walked and entered the temple with them—walking, leaping, and praising God. And all the people saw him walking and praising God. Then they knew that it was he who sat begging alms at the Beautiful Gate of the temple; and they were filled with wonder and amazement at what had happened to him (Acts 3:1-10 NKJV).

This miracle takes place at the gate called Beautiful, where a man crippled from birth is carried daily to beg. As Peter and John approach, he asked them for money. Peter responded with a statement that has echoed for centuries: *"Silver and gold have I none, but what I have I give you: In the name of Jesus Christ of Nazareth, rise up and walk."* Peter takes him by the hand, and immediately strength enters the man's feet and ankles. He leaps up, walking and praising God. The people are astonished, and Peter quickly redirects the glory to Jesus.

This miracle reveals several key truths:

- Miracles flow from what we carry, not what we possess materially.
- Faith is often activated by action—Peter pulled the man up.
- The name of Jesus carries power when spoken in authority.

This healing wasn't just about restoring limbs—it was about establishing the apostolic Church's credibility and proclaiming the resurrection power of Christ. The once-begging man became a walking, leaping testimony. His testimony was too powerful to ignore.

PAUL BLINDING ELYMAS THE SORCERER

But Elymas the sorcerer (for so his name is translated) withstood them, seeking to turn the proconsul away from the faith. Then Saul, who also is called Paul, filled with the Holy Spirit, looked intently at him and said, "O full of all deceit and all fraud, you son of the devil, you

> enemy of all righteousness, will you not cease perverting the straight ways of the Lord? And now, indeed, the hand of the Lord is upon you, and you shall be blind, not seeing the sun for a time." And immediately a dark mist fell on him, and he went around seeking someone to lead him by the hand. Then the proconsul believed, when he saw what had been done, being astonished at the teaching of the Lord (Acts 13:8-12 NKJV).

In Cyprus, Paul and Barnabas faced serious opposition from Elymas, a Jewish sorcerer who tried to turn the proconsul away from faith. Paul, filled with the Holy Spirit, rebukes Elymas and declares that he will be blind for a time. Immediately, darkness falls upon him, and he gropes for someone to lead him by the hand.

This act is not vindictive—it is judicial. Elymas stood against the gospel, and God uses Paul to remove the obstruction by divine authority. The proconsul, witnessing this power, believes.

This miracle underscores:

- The authority of the Church to confront and overpower demonic opposition.
- The role of miracles not only in healing but also in judgment.
- The discernment and boldness that flows from being filled with the Holy Spirit.

Paul's confrontation shows that apostolic power is not passive. It discerns, confronts, and declares in alignment with God's purpose.

HANDKERCHIEF MIRACLES

> Now God worked unusual miracles by the hands of Paul, so that even handkerchiefs or aprons were brought from his body to the sick, and the diseases left them and the evil spirits went out of them (Acts 19:11-12 NKJV).

In Ephesus, God performed extraordinary miracles through the hands of Paul. So tangible was the anointing on him that even handkerchiefs and aprons touched by him are brought to the sick and demon-possessed, and they are healed and delivered.

AN INSANE BOY IS GLORIOUSLY DELIVERED!

I remember in 1997, God used me in a spectacular miracle of healing involving an 18-year-old young man in Saint Lucia, who had recently gone mad. The boy became insanely violent, so they locked him in his bedroom and chained his legs to the bed so he could not hurt anyone or himself.

The boy's father was a very prominent businessman on the island of Saint Lucia. The steering committee of the crusade who was hosting me, brought the father to my hotel room. I led him to the Lord and then talked to him about his child, who was insane. He was very anxious for me to go to his house and pray for the boy. I really wanted to, but the Holy Spirit restrained me and told me not to go. Instead, the Holy Spirit told me to simply pray over an handkerchief and have the man lay it on his son's forehead and God would deliver him from all the demons.

At first the businessman, who came from a staunch Roman Catholic background, was very skeptical, but out of sheer desperation, he obeyed me and went to his house with a handkerchief that I had anointed and prayed over. When he placed the handkerchief on his son's forehead, he said what happened next shocked him—surprised and blessed him at the same time. The power of God came upon his son and drove out all the demons of insanity. The son was gloriously delivered by the power of God, without me being physically present! Glory to God.

This phenomenon reveals the transferable nature of the anointing. Objects become carriers of divine power—not because of superstition, but because of proximity to a Spirit-filled vessel.

These miracles highlight:

- God's desire to reach people even through unconventional means.
- The contagious nature of the Holy Spirit's presence.
- The expanding impact of ministry beyond physical proximity.

This passage in Acts 19:11-12 echoes the ministry of Jesus, where people were healed by touching His garments (Mark 5:30). Now, through the apostles, that same flow of power continued—affirming the ongoing authority of the Church over the powers of darkness.

POWER AND AUTHORITY TRANSFERRED THROUGH THE CHURCH

> Behold, I give you the authority to trample on serpents and scorpions, and over all the power of the enemy, and nothing shall by any means hurt you (Luke 10:19 NKJV).

Together, these miracles form a picture of the Church as an empowered, active agent of divine power:

- Healing the lame shows restoration.
- Blinding the sorcerer shows judgment and protection of truth.
- Handkerchiefs show multiplication and reach.

The Church is not merely a gathering of believers—it is the living body of Christ. Jesus declared in Matthew 28:18-20 that all authority in Heaven and earth was given to Him—and He commissioned His followers to go and conquer the world in that authority. The miracles in the book Acts are evidence that the transfer was real.

The Holy Spirit is the Administrator of this divine authority. At Pentecost, the Holy Spirit filled the believers in the upper room, and from that point forward, they carried and released power wherever they went. Whether speaking healing, confronting darkness, or touching lives remotely, the Church acted as Christ's representatives here on earth.

Today, the Church still bears this mantle. Authority has not ceased. The same Spirit who worked through Peter, Paul, and the early believers indwells every born-again follower of Christ. The miraculous is not for show but for the glory of God and the advancement of His Kingdom. Are you willing to pay the price for the working of miracles in your life?

The Bible stories plus my story of working miracles in this chapter are to challenge believers to recognize what they carry. We may not all walk in the apostolic office, but we carry the same Spirit who raised Jesus from the dead. In Jesus' name, healing still flows, darkness is still expelled, and power still moves—not because we are great, but because greater is He who is in us than he (satan) who is in the world.

The Church is more than a people—it is a power-filled movement, anointed and commissioned to continue what Jesus began. Let us walk in that authority with boldness, faith, and surrender.

PRAYER OF ACTIVATION

Almighty Father, God of Power and Dominion, I come before Your throne of grace in the mighty name of Jesus Christ, declaring that all authority in Heaven and on earth belongs to Him—and that He has delegated that authority to His Church. Your Word declares in Acts 5:12 (NKJV) that "through the hands of the apostles many signs and wonders were done among the people." Today, I take my place in Christ, not as a mere believer but as an authorized ambassador of Your Kingdom, called to enforce Heaven's will on earth through the working of miracles.

Lord Jesus, Risen King and Captain of the Church, You have given me power to heal the sick, cast out devils, and proclaim liberty to the captives. Just as Peter and John said, "What I do have I give you: In the Name of Jesus Christ of Nazareth, rise up and walk," I now declare that what You have placed in me is enough to bring healing, deliverance, and restoration to the nations. I renounce fear, doubt, and passivity. I step boldly into the authority You have entrusted to me, knowing that it is not by might, nor by power, but by Your Spirit.

Holy Spirit, Administrator of Divine Power, fill me afresh with Your fire and boldness. Empower me with keen discernment like Paul who confronted Elymas, and with unwavering faith like Peter who lifted the lame man to his feet. Let the same anointing that flowed through Paul's handkerchiefs flow through my words, my touch, and every work of my hands. Let even the atmosphere around me carry Your power to heal the sick and drive out demons. Make me a living extension of Christ's authority on earth.

By faith, I activate this apostolic dimension of the working of miracles:

- *I decree that the authority of Christ flows through me to heal, deliver, and restore.*
- *I declare that the power of the Holy Spirit is transferable through my yielded life, touching people near and far.*
- *I proclaim that signs and wonders will follow the preaching of the Word from my lips.*
- *I declare that demonic opposition will be judged and removed when I speak under the unction of the Spirit.*
- *I decree that faith will rise wherever I go, and Jesus alone will receive all glory.*

Father, in the name of Jesus, I release healing to the sick, liberty to the captives, and life to the dead places. I command every spiritual Elymas to be blinded and silenced. I send forth the anointed Word, and I declare that even through cloth, prayer cloths, and unseen means, Your power will travel and set the oppressed free.

Lord, make me a sign and a wonder. Let miracles be the evidence that Christ lives in me. Use me to glorify Your name and advance Your Kingdom with apostolic power, boldness, and purity of heart.

I receive by faith this activation into apostolic miracles and divine authority.

In Jesus' mighty name, amen.

12

FAITH, MYSTERY, AND THE GOD WHO STILL WORKS WONDERS

For I will not dare to speak of any of those things which Christ has not accomplished through me, in word and deed, to make the Gentiles obedient—in mighty signs and wonders, by the power of the Spirit of God, so that from Jerusalem and round about to Illyricum I have fully preached the gospel of Christ

(Romans 15:18-19 NKJV).

As we conclude this journey through the miraculous works of God from Genesis to the book of Acts, we must return to the theological foundation underpinning it all—*faith.* Miracles are not random bursts of divine energy. They are signs, wonders, and manifestations of God's power—activated in the atmosphere of faith for the purpose of glorifying Christ.

Two passages, Romans 15:18-19 and Galatians 3:5, provide profound insights into the mechanism by which miracles operate and the divine-human partnership that makes them possible.

Paul writes in Romans 15:18-19 (ESV), *"I will not venture to speak of anything except what Christ has accomplished through me…by word and deed, by the power of signs and wonders, by the power of the Spirit of God…."* Here we see that apostolic ministry is not merely a proclamation of doctrine—it is a demonstration of divine power.

Likewise, Galatians 3:5 (NIV) poses a rhetorical question: *"…does God give you his Spirit and work miracles among you by the works of the law, or by your believing what you heard?"* The answer is clear—miracles flow from faith, not merit.

THE INSTRUMENT OF FAITH

> But without faith it is impossible to please Him, for he who comes to God must believe that He is, and that He is a rewarder of those who diligently seek Him (Hebrews 11:6 NKJV).

Faith is not a religious feeling—it is a conviction that God is who He says He is and will do what He has promised. Hebrews 11:6 declares that without faith it is impossible to please God. Faith is the currency of Heaven, the medium through which God's invisible power is made visible on earth.

In the miracles of Jesus and the apostles, faith was often the prerequisite to the miracles, signs, and wonders they performed. "Your faith has made you whole." "Do you believe I can do this?" These were not casual inquiries. Each were invitations to engage with God's power.

> O foolish Galatians! Who has bewitched you that you should not obey the truth, before whose eyes Jesus Christ was clearly portrayed among you as crucified? This only I want to learn from you: Did you receive the Spirit by the works of the law, or by the hearing of faith? Are you so foolish? Having begun in the Spirit, are you now being made perfect by the flesh? Have you suffered so many things in vain—if indeed it was in vain? Therefore He who supplies the Spirit to you and works miracles among you, does He do it by the works of the law, or by the hearing of faith? (Galatians 3:1-5 NKJV)

Galatians 3:5 highlights that miracles are not the result of legalistic obedience or spiritual striving. They are the fruit of faith—of hearing the Word, believing it, and acting upon it. So much so that the apostle Paul calls any movement away from faith "bewitched." Faith aligns us with God's will and positions us to receive what only He can give. The law of faith controls supply and demand in the Kingdom of God, especially in the world of miracles.

THE ROLE OF THE HOLY SPIRIT

> So he answered and said to me: "This is the word of the Lord to Zerubbabel: 'Not by might nor by power, but by My Spirit,' says the Lord of hosts" (Zechariah 4:6 NKJV).

Romans 15 makes it clear that miracles are not sourced from human effort but in the power of the Holy Spirit. The Spirit is the One who empowers, reveals, and executes God's will on earth. When Paul speaks of signs and wonders, he ties them directly to the Spirit's activity, not his own ingenuity. Every worker of miracles must embrace this level of humility.

This is critical: the Church is not the source of miracles—she is the conduit. The Spirit uses yielded vessels to manifest the supernatural. As we walk in obedience and faith, the Spirit flows through us to accomplish God's purpose. Thus, miracles are Trinitarian in nature: they originate from the will of the Father, are mediated through the name of the Son, and executed by the power of the Holy Spirit. The believer's role is to believe, obey, and make room for God to move.

MIRACLES AS TESTIMONY, NOT ENTERTAINMENT

Paul's words in Romans also remind us that signs and wonders are not for spectacle—they are for testimony. They confirm the Word preached and reveal the reality of the Kingdom of God. Miracles are not ends in themselves but signposts pointing to Jesus.

In a world fascinated with the sensational, the Church must guard the sacredness of the miraculous. True miracles glorify Christ, edify the Church, and convict the lost. When miracles happen apart from the gospel message, they risk becoming distractions. But when they accompany the preaching of Christ crucified and risen, they become tools of transformation.

This is why I personally don't like flowing in healing or miracles before teaching the Word of God. I don't want the people to think I am special or that it's magic.

THEOLOGICAL BALANCE: FAITH, NOT FORMULA

Finally, we must recognize that miracles are not mechanical. There is no formula that guarantees a miracle. Faith is not a lever we pull to force God's hand—it is a surrender that trusts Him to act according to His will. Sometimes miracles are immediate. Sometimes they are delayed.

Sometimes they don't occur the way we expect. But faith remains. Our trust is not in an outcome but in a Person. As Shadrach, Meshach, and Abednego said in Daniel 3:17-18 (NKJV), *"...our God whom we serve is able to deliver us...but if not, we do not serve your gods...."* And Job said with conviction, *"Though He slay me, yet will I trust Him. Even so, I will defend my own ways before Him* (Job 13:15 NKJV).

This is mature faith—a faith that believes for the miraculous but remains anchored in worship regardless of what happens. This is the faith that pleases God and creates an atmosphere where the miraculous can thrive. Miracles are not the center of the gospel—Christ is. However, miracles are the evidence that Christ lives, reigns, and works through His Church.

Romans 15 and Galatians 3 call us back to this essential truth: *the power of God moves through those who believe.* As we reflect on the stories of divine intervention—from the parted seas to resurrected lives—may we not merely admire them but seek to live in the same posture of faith and dependence. The God of miracles is still at work, still speaking, still healing, and still saving. Let us therefore walk in faith, be filled with the Spirit, and expect the supernatural—not for our glory, but for His.

Become a worker of miracles, in Jesus' name!

LIFE APPLICATION SECTION

Memory Verse

For I will not dare to speak of any of those things which Christ has not accomplished through me, in word and deed, to make the Gentiles obedient—in mighty signs and wonders, by the power of the Spirit of God, so that from Jerusalem and round about to Illyricum I have fully preached the gospel of Christ (Romans 15:18-19 NKJV).

Reflections

1. What is the role of the Holy Spirit in the working of miracles?

2. Why did Paul accuse the Galatians of being bewitched?

PRAYER OF ACTIVATION

Heavenly Father, God of Wonders and Glory, I come boldly to Your throne in the name of Jesus Christ, acknowledging that all miracles flow from Your sovereign will, are accomplished by Your Spirit, and are received through faith. Your Word declares in Romans 15:19 (NKJV) that by "mighty signs and wonders, by the power of the Spirit of God…I have fully preached the gospel of Christ." Lord, I surrender my striving, my formulas, and my pride, and I take hold of the law of faith. I believe that You are who You say You are and will do what You have promised.

Lord Jesus Christ, Author and Finisher of my Faith, You are the same yesterday, today, and forever. You healed the sick, raised the dead, and calmed storms—and You now live in me by Your Spirit. Galatians 3:5 declares that You work miracles not by the works of the law, but by the hearing of faith. Today, I choose to hear and believe. I silence the voice of fear, doubt, and unbelief, and I align my heart with the living Word of God. Let my life testify that faith is the atmosphere where Your power moves.

Holy Spirit, Power of the Most High, fill me afresh with Your fire and wonder. Flow through me as a willing vessel—not by might nor by power, but by Your Spirit. I renounce every attempt to manipulate the miraculous or to treat Your power as a formula. I yield to You fully, knowing that I am not the source, but the conduit. Use my hands, my voice, my presence, and my prayers to manifest the will of the Father and the name of the Son.

By faith, I activate this dimension of the working of miracles:

- *I declare that faith will be my operating system, not fear or fleshly striving.*
- *I decree that the Holy Spirit will work mightily through me, confirming the Word with signs and wonders.*
- *I proclaim that miracles will glorify Christ, not people, and testify of His resurrection power.*
- *I declare that my faith will remain anchored in God's character, not in visible results.*

- *I choose to expect the supernatural while worshipping unconditionally, trusting God whether He answers now, later, or in ways I cannot understand.*

Father, in the mighty name of Jesus, I speak life into impossible situations. I call forth healings, deliverances, breakthroughs, and creative miracles as living testimonies of Your Kingdom. Let mighty signs and wonders follow the preaching of the gospel through my life. Make me a living altar where faith and fire meet, and where Your glory is revealed.

I receive by faith this mantle for the working of miracles—not by might, not by power, but by Your Spirit.

In Jesus' name, amen.

ABOUT FRANCIS MYLES

Dr. Francis Myles is a multi-gifted international motivational speaker, business consultant, and apostle to the nations. He is the senior pastor of Jesus Festival Global Church in Fayetteville, Georgia, and in Lusaka, Zambia. He is also the creator and founder of the world's first Marketplace Bible and founder of Francis Myles International (francismyles.com), a TV and multimedia ministry based in Atlanta, Georgia, USA.

Dr. Myles is a sought-after conference speaker in both ministerial and marketplace seminars. He is also a spiritual life coach to "movers and shakers" in the marketplace and political arena. He has appeared on *TBN, GodTV,* and *Daystar,* and has been a featured guest on Sid Roth's *It's Supernatural!* TV show and "This Is Your Day" with Pastor Benny Hinn.

Dr. Myles is happily married to the love of his life, Carmela Real Myles, and they reside in McDonough, a suburb of Atlanta, Georgia.

In the Right Hands, This Book Will Change Lives!

Most of the people who need this message will not be looking for this book. To change their lives, you need to **put a copy of this book in their hands.**

Our ministry is constantly seeking methods to find the people who need this anointed message to change their lives. **Will you help us reach these people?**

Extend this ministry by sowing three, five, ten, or *even more* books today and change people's lives for the better! Your generosity will be part of catalyzing the Great Awakening that many have been prophesying and praying for.

From

Dr. Francis Myles

Tear down unholy altars and close the enemy's entryways into your life!

Do you feel like invisible barriers are keeping you from the life you want? This may be the result of hidden, evil altars in the spirit realm. An "altar" is not simply a physical object used for religious or occultic practice; it's an invisible entry point that grants forces of darkness access to your life by partnering with the enemy.

In *Dangerous Prayers from the Courts of Heaven that Destroy Evil Altars*, Dr. Francis Myles teaches you to tear down these unholy altars, breaking free from many areas of sin and bondage. By praying through a framework of "dangerous prayers," Dr. Myles teaches you to enter the Courts of Heaven and claim Jesus as your legal advocate in the spirit realm.

You don't have to wait another day for someone else to lay hands on you. Take hold of your own deliverance and walk in freedom today!

Purchase your copy wherever books are sold